EXTRAORDINARILY ORDINARY

EXTRAORDINARILY ORDINARY

Us Weekly and the Rise of Reality Television Celebrity

ERIN A. MEYERS

RUTGERS UNIVERSITY PRESS
NEW BRUNSWICK, CAMDEN, AND NEWARK,
NEW JERSEY, AND LONDON

Library of Congress Cataloging-in-Publication Data

Names: Meyers, Erin A., author.
Title: Extraordinarily ordinary : Us weekly and the rise of reality television celebrity / Erin Meyers.
Description: New Brunswick : Rutgers University Press, 2020. | Includes bibliographical refrerences and index.
Identifiers: LCCN 2019016324 | ISBN 9780813599427 (paperback) | ISBN 9780813599434 (cloth) | ISBN 9780813599441 (ePUB) | ISBN 9780813599458 (mobi) | ISBN 9780813599465 (web PDF)
Subjects: LCSH: Reality television programs—Social aspects—United States. | Celebrities—United States. | Television personalities—United States. | Us weekly.
Classification: LCC PN1992.8.R43 M49 2020 | DDC 791.45/750922—dc23
LC record available at https://lccn.loc.gov/2019016324

A British Cataloging-in-Publication record for this book is available from the British Library.

∞ The paper used in this publication meets the requirements of the American National Standard for Information Sciences—Permanence of Paper for Printed Library Materials, ANSI Z39.48-1992.

www.rutgersuniversitypress.org

Manufactured in the United States of America

CONTENTS

EXTRAORDINARILY ORDINARY

INTRODUCTION

The notion of "celebrity" has infiltrated every part of twenty-first-century popular and media cultures. Like a train wreck—a metaphor tellingly used to describe those celebrities whose excessive behaviors are regularly featured in mainstream and entertainment news outlets—it is hard to look away from the ongoing sagas of celebrities as their private lives are exhaustingly documented across mass media. Celebrity gossip weeklies line the grocery store checkout lines and airport kiosks, enticing readers with glossy photos and sensational headlines that promise an inside look at the "real" person behind the celebrity facade. This obsession with the real and the increased competition among gossip weeklies to bring audiences the inside scoop have transformed celebrity culture by expanding the range of individuals whose real lives fascinate us. According to the *Wall Street Journal*, "people who owe their fame to reality TV accounted for about 40% of the covers of the six major celebrity weekly magazines in 2011" (Adams, 2012, p. D1). From *Teen Moms* to *Real Housewives* to, of course, the Kardashians (sisters Kim, Khloé, and Kourtney and their mother, Kris, from *Keeping Up with the Kardashians*)—who in 2011 were "the subject of about one of every six celebrity weekly stories" and were top-five sellers for four of the six major gossip weekly titles—editors increasingly turned to reality stars precisely because of their willingness to "tell you every detail about their life" (ibid.). Appearing to acquire fame for doing little more than offer their private lives for public consumption, reality stars are routinely decried as valueless celebrities who are simply "famous for being famous." Yet, as these magazine sales numbers suggest, reality television celebrities have captured the public's attention, and their rise to cultural prominence speaks to a shift in the ways we think about and engage with celebrity culture in the twenty-first century.

This book offers a critical analysis of the exploding coverage of reality television cast members in *Us Weekly* magazine, the top celebrity weekly of the 2000s, to delineate its role in the production of a distinct form of twenty-first-century celebrity—the extraordinarily ordinary. The extraordinarily ordinary celebrity destabilizes traditional conceptions of celebrity in multiple ways: by challenging how one acquires and maintains fame, by recalibrating the roles of various industrial forces at work in this process, and by closing the cultural distance between the ordinary person and the extraordinary star in ways that intensify that celebrity's cultural role as markers of social identity, particularly gender, race, class, and sexuality. *Us Weekly*'s construction of the extraordinarily ordinary celebrity within its gossip narratives is a significant symptom of the broader intensification of discourses of ordinariness in the production of contemporary celebrity, in which fame is paradoxically grounded in "just being yourself" while simultaneously defining what the "right" sort of self is in contemporary culture. Thus, if the reality television celebrity is valorized (or denigrated) for just being herself, what sort of self matters? And how and why does the celebrity industry, particularly celebrity gossip media, help validate a particular view of the self through the attention to ordinariness?

Tracing the rise of the reality television celebrity as extraordinarily ordinary is an attempt to both historicize the broader shift toward ordinariness within contemporary celebrity culture and delineate its continued impact on even newer forms of celebrity, such as the "microcelebrities" originating from such platforms as YouTube, Twitter, and Instagram (Senft, 2008; Marwick 2013; Marwick & boyd, 2011). Engaging the tools of digital media to construct and promote their own personas directly to their target audiences, YouTubers, Instagram Influencers, and other social media celebrities offer the same "illusion—often exemplified by the success of reality television stars—that anyone can be famous" because these personas are built on the successful performance of the private and ordinary self rather than a more traditional claim to talent or skill (Khamis, Ang, & Welling, p. 194). Though social media celebrities have seemingly done an end run around the traditional gatekeepers of celebrity culture, like *Us Weekly* and other celebrity gossip weeklies that were a necessary part of the rise of reality television celebrity, their performances of the authentic and ordinary self are rooted in the same presentational labors that defined the extraordinarily ordinary celebrity in traditional gossip media. By foregrounding the attention-getting performances of the ordinary and private self that are the hallmark of constructing the reality television cast member as a celebrity, *Us Weekly*'s coverage helped set the stage for the work of self-branding or of "the presentation of oneself as a celebrity regardless of who is paying attention" that is at the core of the social media microcelebrity (Marwick, 2013, p. 114).

This book begins from a premise that, as Richard Dyer (1986) and others have suggested, stars are markers of what it means to be human at a particular time and place and, as such, reveal deeper ideas about who we are and how we see ourselves in this cultural moment. As will be argued throughout this book, the turn toward ordinariness that is central to the rise of the reality television celebrity is not simply a story about expanding celebrity culture but about how to be a person in contemporary society. Joshua Gamson (2011) suggests: "The ordinary turn in celebrity culture is ultimately part of a heightened consciousness of everyday life as a public performance—and increased expectation that we are being watched, a growing willingness to offer up private parts of the self to watchers known and unknown, and a hovering sense that perhaps the unwatched life is invalid or insufficient" (p. 1068). Emerging at the cusp of the digital age, the extraordinarily ordinary celebrity as constructed in *Us Weekly*, I argue, is a key figure in what P. David Marshall (2010) suggests is celebrity culture's pedagogical role in the transition from a representational culture to presentational culture in which "the organisation and production of the on-line self . . . has become at the very least an important component of our presentation of ourselves to the world" (p. 39). Bringing the intimate and private self into the realm of the public, reality television began and social media continue to encourage all of us to do the work of creating a persona, to highlight the "best" part of ourselves, and to perform the "right" sort of identity to earn attention and value within culture.

Changing Media Landscapes: Reality Television and Celebrity Weeklies

Reality television, with its emphasis on capturing the often ordinary and quotidian events of "real" life, is a media genre explicitly concerned with the revelation of the private and ordinary individual for public consumption. Reality television's textual characteristics rest on a "self-conscious claim to the discourse of the real," even though such discourses are knowingly mediated through a camera and manipulated by producers and editors (Murray & Ouelette, 2004, p. 2). Throughout the history of television, numerous genres, including game shows, talk shows, and documentaries, have brought "real" people, as opposed to media professionals (including existing celebrities), into our living rooms (Grindstaff, 2011; Hill, 2015; Holmes, 2004a). Although reality-based programming has always had a presence on television, the genre experienced massive expansion in the late 1990s and early 2000s beginning with the global successes of *Big Brother* and *Survivor* (Hill, 2005). With cheap-to-produce, easily replicable, and globally exportable formats, reality programming quickly proliferated across cable and broadcast television in ways that reshaped the television landscape and popular culture more broadly around discourse of "the real."

In January 2003, the *New York Times* declared, "Executives from all four major networks watched in awe as reality shows won 15 of 18 half hour time periods on Monday, Tuesday, and Wednesday nights" and "were now ready to embrace plans for a radical restructuring of the network business" around the year-round production of reality programming to better compete with cable and counter sagging ratings for scripted television (Carter, 2003, p. A1; Frutkin, 2004). This "radical restructuring" proved successful, as according to a Nielsen analysis of ratings data from 2000–2010, reality television dominated prime-time ratings throughout the decade. Beginning in the 2002–2003 television season, reality television "consistently captured the largest percentage of the audience watching the top ten broadcast programs" (Nielsen, 2011, para. 2). The genre routinely averaged over half of the total audience viewing those programs, peaking in the 2007–2008 season with 77.3 percent of the prime-time top-ten audience. In particular, the genre drew coveted young viewers, "who have watched reality shows in far bigger numbers than anything else on television" (Carter, 2003, p. C14). As the decade progressed, the sheer number of reality programs exploded, and by 2010 the reality genre accounted for 40 percent of U.S. television's prime-time schedule (across cable and broadcast), with around six hundred different series airing during that year (Barnhart, 2010). Cable, in particular, doubled down on the format, with entire channels, such as Bravo, TruTV, and VH1, basing all or nearly all of their schedules around reality programming. The 2000s, then, are an important decade in which to begin to historicize reality television and the celebrities that emerged from it.

While reality television narratives are built around claims to the "real," audiences are not merely dupes who believe everything shown on reality television is true or the personalities authentic, and much of the pleasure in watching reality television comes from the negotiation of fact and fiction (Hill, 2005). It is this process of negotiation, however, that helps reaffirm the real within reality television, as audiences seek the truth about the everyday cast members through their strategies of belief and disbelief (Ouellette & Murray, 2004). Tellingly, this sort of negotiation parallels the negotiation of public/private and artifice/authenticity that drives celebrity gossip media, whose concurrent expansion was, it will be argued in this book, tied to the rise of reality television. According to the *New York Times*, the average total sales of the popular celebrity weeklies *Star*,[1] *People*, *Us Weekly*, and *In Touch* combined were up 11.6 percent at the end of 2004, with *Star* and *In Touch* sales each rising about 80 percent from the previous year (Story, 2005). Surging subscription and single-issue sales across the genre led to the introduction of new titles eager to tap into this growing market, including *Life & Style Weekly* in 2004 and a U.S. version of British celebrity weekly *OK!* in 2005. The celebrity weekly is a glossy, colorful, and photo-filled print magazine devoted exclusively to the coverage of celebrities—their work and, more centrally, their off-screen lives. Like reality television, celebrity weeklies are centered on the public display of the real and private self. These magazines trade in gossip, using paparazzi photos of celebrities in their unguarded moments and intimate tidbits about their real lives to promote an intimate relationship between the reader and the celebrity. They alternate between reveling in the glamour of celebrity lifestyles and humanizing celebrities, promising the reader that they are just like us. Aimed primarily at a young (eighteen to thirty-four) female audience, these magazines offer an overwhelmingly positive, if at times cheeky, take on the life and times of celebrities. *Us Weekly* is an important artifact for analysis, as it was during the early to mid-2000s that the title became one of the top selling U.S. celebrity weeklies by establishing a distinct and much-copied tone and style that offered a frothy blend of ordinary and extraordinary discourses. Reality television cast members fit neatly into this formula, and their presence proliferated across the magazine. But such coverage of reality television cast members did more than just fill pages. It also helped validate the performance of (the right kind of) ordinariness, or just being yourself, as a viable path to fame in ways that resonated across celebrity culture.

A Brief History of *Us Weekly*

Originally founded by the New York Times Company in 1977 as a general entertainment magazine, *Us Weekly* was purchased by Wenner Media, headed by *Rolling Stone* founder Jann Wenner, in 1985. It was published as a monthly title until Wenner transformed it into a more "style-oriented" and celebrity-friendly weekly in 1999 in an attempt to boost its sales and challenge the industry leaders *People* and *Entertainment Weekly* (Kuczynski, 1999; Snider, 2017). This rebranding was not, however, an immediate success in terms of overall circulation. Setting an ambitious average single-copy circulation target of 700,000 at the mid-March 2000 launch of the revamped title, Wenner amended that target to 300,000 and slashed ad pages almost in half by the July 3 issue (Fine, 2000). As the year progressed, the magazine struggled to define its brand and connect with readers until Wenner made two key decisions. First, he sold Disney a 50 percent stake in the magazine in February 2001 to help alleviate larger financial burdens within the company and to give *Us Weekly* the benefit of the large conglomerate's promotional networks (Kuczynski, 2001). As part of the deal, the magazine was "heavily cross-promoted by other Disney properties, especially ABC shows such as *The View* and *Good Morning America*" and, in turn, began to heavily cover celebrities with ties to Disney programming, notably the cast members of the ABC reality franchise *The Bachelor* (Hayes, 2001). While Disney chairman Michael Eisner and Jan Wenner both stressed that the magazine would "retain its editorial independence within the Disney empire" and thus not be focused solely on Disney-related content, it was clear that both Wenner Media and Disney saw the partnership as an opportunity to attract a coveted young female audience (Colford, 2001, p. 24).

On the heels of the sale to Disney, Wenner's second pivotal move was to introduce an editorial shift that would come to redefine *Us Weekly* and, subsequently, the celebrity weekly genre in general. In February 2002, Bonnie Fuller—the former editor of the women's magazines *Marie Claire*, *Cosmopolitan*, and

Glamour—was hired to overhaul the magazine and make it more competitive. Fuller established a new brand for the magazine based on what *New York Times* media critic David Carr (2008) described as a "fundamental conceptual scoop: Stars, however stellar they may appear, are just like us—if you don't count the parts about unusually beautiful and impossibly wealthy" (para. 4). The magazine re-emerged with a careful balance of the ordinary and extraordinary, rendered in "a girly template [of] bubbly pastels and embroidered with lots of over-narration about stars' foibles and mortality" (ibid., para. 6). This rebranding was aimed at attracting a young, female audience, supported by what Andrea McDonnell (2014) contends is the celebrity gossip media's "single-minded goal: to document and comment on the personal lives of celebrity women" (p. 7). Essentially, *Us Weekly* became and remains a scrapbook of paparazzi photos of stars' everyday lives running alongside more in-depth articles that further delve into those private and ordinary selves largely through attention to romantic and familial narratives. But stars are also glamorous and special, as the magazine revels in the lavish lifestyles that make the ordinary lives of stars so enviable. Under Fuller's leadership, fashion and beauty became a central theme, with weekly features like Red Carpet, Who Wore It Best, and Star Beauty highlighting the stars as beautiful alongside longer features that peek into celebrity lifestyles—vacations, homes, and beauty regimens that reaffirm celebrity culture's hyperfeminine and consumerist gender norms.

The routine and predictable nature of this content, as well as its mingling of extraordinary and ordinary discourses, is evident in the magazine's editorial calendar, a predetermined "schema of the year, which assigns content to issues in anticipation of pre-selected events, holidays, and topics" (McDonnell, 2014, p. 52). Figure 1 depicts the 2015 publishing schedule for *Us Weekly*. These calendars represent the dominant themes of the issue, though not necessarily the cover story, as developing celebrity gossip and scandal will always be at forefront of the magazine's content. Though I was unable to locate media kits for the years covered by this study, the 2015 calendar illustrates the continuation of a brand established in the early 2000s—namely, a focus on fashion, beauty, and style through a lens of celebrity culture. Celebrity glamour is highlighted through coverage of awards shows and such special issues as "Celebrity Style," "Hollywood's Best Dressed List," and "Us Hot Bodies," while a peek at a more ordinary celebrity lifestyle is foregrounded in features like Hollywood Moms and Food. This calendar also lists the cover date versus the on-sale date for the magazine, a crucial distinction particularly for the promotional narratives discussed in chapter 2. The cover date for *Us Weekly*, which I am using to date all my examples in this study, is ten days after the on-sale date of the magazine. This is a standard practice across the print magazine industry that allows the magazine to continue to appear current during its full time on the newsstand. For *Us Weekly*'s coverage of reality television, this means the covers featuring exclusive details on upcoming

Us WEEKLY

2015 PUBLISHING SCHEDULE

SPECIAL THEMED EDITORIAL FEATURES	ISSUE	COVER DATE	ON-SALE DATE	AD CLOSE/ MATERIALS DUE
Year End/New Year	1038	January 5	December 26	December 8
● HOLLYWOOD'S BEST DIETS	1039	January 12	January 2	December 15
	1040	January 19	January 9	December 22
▲ GOLDEN GLOBE AWARDS/PEOPLE'S CHOICE AWARDS	1041	January 26	January 16	December 29
	1042	February 2	January 23	January 5
▲ SAG AWARDS/PRE-SUPERBOWL/VALENTINE'S DAY	1043	February 9	January 30	January 12
Post-Superbowl	1044	February 16	February 6	January 19
▲ GRAMMY AWARDS	1045	February 23	February 13	January 26
	1046	March 2	February 20	February 2
▲ OSCAR'S AWARDS/INDEPENDENT SPIRIT AWARDS	1047	March 9	February 27	February 9
	1048	March 16	March 6	February 16
Hollywood's Best Dressed List	1049	March 23	March 13	February 23
	1050	March 30	March 20	March 2
● YEAR'S BEST MAKEOVERS	1051	April 6	March 27	March 9
Kids Choice Awards* (TBD)	1052	April 13	April 3	March 16
Celebrity Health & Fitness	1053	April 20	April 10	March 23
MTV Movie Awards	1054	April 27	April 17	March 30
Academy of Country Music Awards (ACMA's)	1055	May 4	April 24	April 6
Mother's Day Gift Guide	1056	May 11	May 1	April 13
	1057	May 18	May 8	April 20
Countdown to Summer	1058	May 25	May 15	April 27
● US HOT BODIES/CANNES FILM FESTIVAL/BILLBOARD MUSIC AWARDS	1059	June 1	May 22	May 4
Cannes Film Festival /Summer TV Preview	1060	June 8	May 29	May 11
Father's Day Gift Guide	1061	June 15	June 5	May 18
	1062	June 22	June 12	May 25
	1063	June 29	June 19	June 1
	1064	July 6	June 26	June 8
	1065	July 13	July 3	June 15
	1066	July 20	July 10	June 22
	1067	July 27	July 17	June 29
	1068	August 3	July 24	July 6
Teen Choice Awards*	1069	August 10	July 31	July 13
● HOLLYWOOD MOMS/BACK-TO-SCHOOL**	1070	August 17	August 7	July 20
	1071	August 24	August 14	July 27
	1072	August 31	August 21	August 3
	1073	September 7	August 28	August 10
● CELEBRITY STYLE** ▲ MTV VMA's*	1074	September 14	September 4	August 17
● FALL TV ISSUE**/FASHION WEEK	1075	September 21	September 11	August 24
Fashion Week	1076	September 28	September 18	August 31
▲ PRIMETIME EMMYS	1077	October 5	September 25	September 7
	1078	October 12	October 2	September 14
Home/Food/Entertaining	1079	October 19	October 9	September 21
Celebrity Health & Fitness	1080	October 26	October 16	September 28
	1081	November 2	October 23	October 5
	1082	November 9	October 30	October 12
Holiday Movie Preview/Babies of the Year	1083	November 16	November 6	October 19
Fall Music Issue**	1084	November 23	November 13	October 26
	1085	November 30	November 20	November 2
Holiday Gift Guide/Celebrity Causes	1086	December 7	November 27	November 9
Holiday Entertaining	1087	December 14	December 4	November 16
Holiday Last Minute Gift Guide	1088	December 21	December 11	November 23
	1089	December 28	December 18	November 30

● US WEEKLY FRANCHISE ▲ MAJOR AWARD SHOWS ISSUES

2.6.15 All issue dates subject to change. *Awards Shows- air date subject to change **Us Franchise issue dates are subject to change until dates are officially approved. Insertion orders are contracted by issue date not edit content. Cover positions and special units (gatefolds, inserts, scent strips, etc.) close 30 days prior. Cover positions and special units in Awards / Franchise Issues ad close 60 days prior. All orders non-cancellable upon closing date.

Figure 1. *Us Weekly* 2015 publishing schedule. Retrieved June 8, 2018 from https://www.usmagazine.com/mediakits-print-editorial-calendar/.

episodes are published before or as the episode airs, even though the cover date is after the airdate of the episode.

In addition to this glossy look at celebrity lifestyles, a second essential component of *Us Weekly*'s genre-defining style was a more serious emphasis on exclusivity and access, promising readers truth over rumor and defining celebrity news rather than responding to it. As the *Vanity Fair* media bloggers Lindsey Weber and Bobby Finger (2017) write, "instead of resorting to filling its pages with recycled rumors printed by its competition, [*Us Weekly*] would come up with creative ways to skirt what could only be considered a [perceived] 'lack of access'" (para. 9). These "creative ways," according to Weber and Finger, helped to promote the intimate relationship with the celebrity through the emphasis on harmless rather than scandalous private-side discourses best embodied by the Stars!—They're Just Like *Us*! photos that appear in every issue. Through paparazzi photos of stars taking out the trash or walking their dogs, readers are brought close to celebrities, further intensifying their roles as markers of how to be an individual in contemporary society (Dyer, 1986). Under the editorial direction of Janice Min, a Columbia University School of Journalism graduate who served first as executive editor under Bonnie Fuller and became editor in chief after Fuller's departure in 2003, the magazine focused on original reporting rather than simply responding to the latest gossip. In contrast to a tabloid's conventional position of outsider in the circuit of celebrity production, *Us Weekly* sought to legitimate itself by leveraging its insider and often direct access to the star as evidence of its cultural power. Cover stories are often accompanied with the headline "Exclusive" or "Only in *Us*," to advise the reader that the magazine has the real story that will not be reported elsewhere and thus serves as an enticement to buy *Us* over a competitor. In the case of reality television coverage, this often is framed as "what you didn't see on TV," positioning the magazine, not the program, as the source for the real ordinary individual. Together, Fuller and Min successfully rebranded *Us Weekly* as a weekly glimpse at the everyday lives of stars, with an emphasis on fashion/beauty, relationships, and scandal, all wrapped in a veneer of truth and authenticity reinforced by proximity to celebrities but still with enough distance to lovingly mock their foibles.

Fuller's takeover was remarkably successful from the start, with 2002's single-copy sales jumping 55.2 percent and overall circulation that year surging to 1.1 million from 2000's circulation rate of 827,363 (Fine, 2003). This growth continued under Min's leadership, and the magazine boasted a circulation rate of 1.9 million at the end of her tenure in 2009 (Abramowitz, 2009). While Min may have led the magazine to industry dominance "on tracks already laid down by Ms. Fuller," she honed the magazine's brand and established it as not only an industry leader but a cultural powerhouse that set the bar for celebrity weeklies throughout the decade. Though Min herself has said she had little interest in celebrity culture, having never, for instance, "watched an episode of *The Bachelor*," her keen eye for figuring out what audiences wanted helped drive the magazine to the heights of success (WNYC Studios, 2018). Amy Vincinguerra, who served as deputy managing editor under Min, described Min's "special gift" as her ability to "take something that exists and make it way better. . . . Janice had a knack—and our whole team had a knack under her leadership—of delivering the reader what they never knew they always wanted" (Sharpe, 2017). In the first year of Min's editorial leadership, the magazine's newsstand sales rose 47.3 percent to 745,887, ad pages grew 25.2 percent, and *Us Weekly* was named *Advertising Age*'s Magazine of the Year (Fine, 2004). Anointing her Editor of the Year in 2005, *Adweek* noted Min's "sprinkling of stardust is not so much how she's positioned the magazine as how she's positioned the celebrities themselves" (*Adweek* staff, 2005, para. 14). Min reshaped *Us Weekly* and, by extension, celebrity culture around ordinariness, saying, "My generation thinks of celebrities as their peers—like neighbors, or people you went to high school with. . . . They're on a first-name basis with them" (ibid.). I argue it was this emphasis on presenting stars as "Just Like *Us!*" that made *Us Weekly* an ideal vehicle for the promotion of reality cast members whose ordinariness was at the very core of their public personas and transforming them into extraordinarily ordinary celebrities.

Reality Celebrity and *Us Weekly*

Given the popularity of the reality television genre in the early twenty-first century, it is not particularly surprising that celebrity weeklies also expanded to include reality television cast members. Celebrity weeklies are a genre focused on the entertainment industry, and the rising popularity of reality television programming simply opened a new avenue for magazine content that reflected contemporary trends in popular culture. Vincinguerra noted the importance of reality television to *Us*'s ascendency, saying, "This look at celebrity culture and pop culture that *Us* did sort of rose in parallel with the tipping point of reality TV when it went from the early days of *The Real World* and TLC shows to what we have now" (Sharpe, 2017). While Fuller may have set the initial tone for the magazine, my analysis indicates it was Min who pioneered the increased coverage of reality stars in *Us Weekly*, beginning most notably with the cast members of *The Bachelor* and *The Bachelorette*, two Disney-owned television programs (Carr, 2008, para. 24). The increased attention to reality television celebrities fit neatly into the magazine's brand identity first because their images are rooted in private-side discourses and, more importantly, because they are also available to the magazine in ways A-list stars are not. As will be discussed in chapter 2, interviews and other "exclusive" appearances in the magazine are crucial to the promotion of the program, as well as the construction of the reality cast member as a celebrity. By mid-decade, reality stars like Lauren Conrad and Heidi Montag (*The Hills*), Jon and Kate Gosselin (*Jon & Kate Plus 8*), and Trista and Ryan Sutter (*The Bachelorette)* were regularly featured on the magazine's cover, elevating them to a higher celebrity status by virtue of just being themselves in this very public media space.

Reality Television Cover Stories

Covers are essential spaces for quickly and succinctly conveying the magazine's brand and enticing a potential reader to purchase the magazine. Andrea McDonnell (2014) claims, "Everything from the choice of photo and color to the placement of headlines is meticulously considered to not only capture reader attention, but also to maintain the brand identity of the magazine" (p. 53). Particularly for celebrity magazines like *Us Weekly*, covers drive newsstand sales, "which can be half of the total circulation and an important component of revenue" (Carr, 2003, p. C2). The cover serves a crucial economic function for the magazine, soliciting readers who will buy the magazine and promising advertisers access to the eyeballs of these readers. As Ellen McCracken (1993) avers, "if the cover image and text do not succeed in enticing large groups of readers, the reach of the other ads inside will be diminished" (p. 18). Thus, an appealing cover is paramount to the economic function of the magazine, and Vincinguerra said covers were selected during meetings involving both the editorial and business side of the magazine (Sharpe, 2017). But covers are also a tool for solidifying the "ideological positionalities" of the magazine, defining not only who the magazine is for but what those readers (ought to) think about the world and the self (McCracken, 1993, p. 22). This ideological positioning carries through in the content of the magazine itself, helping to establish the magazine within the familiar codes of the genre as well as distinguish it from its competition.

Just as reality television programming was reshaping the television landscape, the ways in which reality television cast members were covered in the magazines, particularly their presence on the covers as the main appeal to pick up the magazine, helped reshape how audiences think about celebrity. Min specifically pointed to reality celebrities as fomenting a larger shift in celebrity culture that influenced (and I argue was influenced by) *Us Weekly* coverage: "Thanks to cable television, reality TV and the Internet, the whole power structure of celebrity has shifted. It's not just that Kim Kardashian is a celebrity and nobody knows why. It's her sister, her mother. Young women in particular have forged a connection with the stars of reality TV that they don't have with Gwyneth Paltrow. The whole relationship dynamic between the general population and celebrity has morphed into a *belief that there's very little separating you from being like them*" (Abramowitz, 2009, para. 6–7, emphasis mine). Min keenly recognized that reality cast members, whose private lives are always already on display, fit neatly into the audience desire to see stars as just like us and thus increasingly covered these individuals in the magazine and routinely placed them on the cover. Over the ten years examined in this study, *Us Weekly* featured reality television cast members as the main cover story sixty-one times (or 11 percent of all covers) and as second-level cover stories eighty-five times. By second-level cover story, I refer to the smaller images and headlines that surround the main larger

Figure 2. *Us Weekly* cover from June 1, 2009, featuring reality television celebrities as part of every story (main story features Kate Gosselin from *Jon & Kate Plus 8*, second-level stories feature the season 3 bachelorette Jennifer Schefft, the season 13 *Bachelor* runner-up [and *Dancing with the Stars* season 8 contestant] Melissa Rycroft, and *The Hills* cast member Audrina Patridge).

image and headline on a particular issue's cover. These stories are not the biggest in the issue but are important enough to put on the cover to entice readers to pick up the magazine. There are typically two or three second-level cover stories included on any given cover, which offers greater opportunity for reality celebrities to be featured. Indeed, in some instances, reality celebrities from different programs were featured in different second-level stories on the same cover. Figure 2 depicts an *Us Weekly* cover where all of the cover stories featured are centered on a reality television cast member.

The presence of reality television and its cast members in *Us Weekly* grew slowly. The early part of the decade saw few covers of *Us Weekly* featuring any reality television coverage, with just three covers during 2002 and only five in 2004, but the covers increasingly featured reality television cast members as the decade progressed. In 2008, for instance, ten main story covers (or 19 percent of the covers for that year) featured reality stars, and in 2009, sixteen main story covers (or 30 percent of the covers for that year) did. By far the most common reality cast members featured on the cover across the time of this study were the various contestants from *The Bachelor* and *The Bachelorette* franchises, with twenty-two main cover stories and thirty-one second-level cover stories appearing between 2002 and 2009. Likewise, and in a span of just three years (2007–2009), the stars of the MTV docusoap *The Hills* appeared as part of the main cover story a total of thirteen times and as a second-level cover story seventeen times, meaning these ordinary young women appeared in some fashion on nearly 30 percent of the covers for these two years. And they were not alone. During these same two years, an additional twenty main story covers and twenty-six second-level covers were devoted to reality celebrities from such programs as *The Bachelor*, *Jon & Kate Plus 8*, *The Girls Next Door*, and, beginning in 2009, *Keeping Up with the Kardashians*. In these final years of the decade, then, nearly half of *Us Weekly* covers featured at least one reality television cast member.

Despite the growing number of covers devoted to reality television cast members, little attention has been paid to the ways in which the reality celebrity functions within celebrity weeklies and the history of the relationship between celebrity weeklies and reality television in the construction and circulation of reality stardom in relation to the "ordinary celebrity." That is, this didn't just happen; rather, the increasing presence of these specific types of stars is tied to the work of various cultural intermediaries whose invisible labor has always been central to the construction and circulation of celebrity images. Following Graeme Turner's (2010) call for celebrity studies to "establish a stronger base for the study of the industrial production of celebrity," this book focuses on the rise of the reality star in gossip magazines as symptomatic of a broader shift toward the ordinary as a core discourse of contemporary celebrity (p. 15). There have been few studies that attempt to historicize concurrent changes within the related media industries as a means to understand the forces of industrial production behind this shift toward the ordinary celebrity. For example, some scholarly work has been done on reality television as a new space of construction and circulation of the ordinary celebrity (Biressi & Nunn, 2006; Couldry, 2002; Curnett, 2011; Holmes, 2004a; Meyers, 2010) but far less attention has been given to the role of the gossip media industry's coverage of reality stars as a component of their ascent to celebrity status. Anne Helen Petersen's (2011) analysis of the *National Enquirer* and *People* magazine during the 1970s is one of the few studies focused on the industrial shifts within the gossip media industry and the impact of such shifts on celebrity culture. She offers a historical analysis of the form, content, and modes of production and distribution of these popular magazines during their rise to cultural prominence during the 1970s, arguing that their success was built on a widening of the category of celebrity to "effectively create an endless stream of 'personality'-based fodder for the publications to exploit" (p. 141). In short, because they helped circulate these images, these publications played a crucial role in shaping who was considered a celebrity, as well as the social values that celebrities embodied during the 1970s. This book aims to build on these earlier works to better theorize the industrial, economic, and social contexts and relationships that contributed to the rise of the extraordinarily ordinary celebrity in the early twenty-first century.

Ephemeral Archives: Researching Celebrity Gossip Media

The primary methods for this book are textual and discursive analyses of reality television celebrities as they appear in the popular U.S. celebrity weekly *Us Weekly*. Despite the popularity of this title, access to back issues is difficult. Given their status as ephemera and "fluff," a cultural designation that contributes to the feminization of the celebrities that emerge from these spaces, few university libraries subscribe to celebrity gossip magazines and even fewer archive them. My home library, Kresge Library at Oakland University, does not even include this title in its popular magazine holdings and has no online access to back issues. The University of Michigan, a nearby large research institution, subscribes to *Us Weekly* for its current popular magazine holdings and archives most old issues for only two years before removing them from the collection. It does have a few issues archived as far back as 2013, but this archive has several issues missing and is thus incomplete. The University of Michigan research librarian I spoke to said this title often "walks away" from the library, making it a challenge to assemble a complete archive (Alex, personal communication). Interestingly, the University of Michigan does maintain online access to an archive of *Us Weekly* dating back to 2000, but this archive is text only. Given the primacy of images to this title's style and ideological framing of celebrity, an online archive of text articles only would offer a very partial view of the magazine's coverage of celebrities. Or, as the University of Michigan research librarian put it, "how boring" (ibid.).

Fortunately, the popular culture periodicals archive at the Ray & Pat Browne Popular Culture Library at Bowling Green State University houses an almost complete archive of *Us Weekly* beginning from March 27, 2000, which was just after Wenner's relaunch of the title. This collection is the most complete print archive of *Us Weekly* available and, while the library does archive other celebrity weeklies, such as *Star* and *In Touch Weekly*, these archives are much less complete than their *Us Weekly* archive.[2] That *Us Weekly* was chosen, among all possible celebrity gossip weekly titles, to be archived by the Ray & Pat Browne Popular Culture library speaks to the magazine's centrality to contemporary celebrity and media cultures. My unprecedented access to a print archive of back issues of *Us Weekly* enables me to trace changes over time and offer a more complete picture of how the coverage of reality celebrities in *Us Weekly* served its industrial and economic goals, as well as disrupted traditional conceptions of stardom.

From this print archive, I created a personal digital archive documenting the appearance of reality television cast members across the magazine, including cover stories, noncover articles, appearances in photo features, and so on.[3] While my digital archive amounted to over 750 separate documents (many of which included multiple pages of content), this book is not intended to be an exhaustive content analysis of every reality star that appeared within the pages of *Us Weekly* during the early 2000s. The goal is not to document every appearance but rather to put the increased presence of these stars within the magazine into a broader context of concurrent shifts within celebrity and media cultures. My archive documents were subsequently organized and inductively coded using MAXQDA qualitative research software to identify the specific reality cast members covered (e.g., who appeared / when / how often / and in what context or section of the magazine) and to establish broader qualitative themes related to the shift from reality cast member to reality celebrity, including the forms of labor that help build celebrity, as well as issues of race, class, gender, and sexuality that shape the performance of such labor. These themes are explored throughout the book as I trace the contours of the extraordinarily ordinary celebrity as a distinct form of celebrity that disrupts traditional conceptions of fame while simultaneously upholding the patriarchal norms that have long defined celebrity culture.

An Overview

This book is divided into four chapters, each of which explores a particular aspect of *Us Weekly*'s role in the emergence of the extraordinarily ordinary celebrity. Chapter 1 unpacks the theoretical concepts of the ordinary/private self and extraordinary/public self that shape traditional scholarly approaches to stardom to trace how the magazine's attention to reality television cast members was a vehicle for the rise of the extraordinarily ordinary celebrity. To reconceptualize traditional notions of stardom to accommodate the reality star as an extraordinarily ordinary celebrity who is famous for "just being herself," this chapter lays out three forms of labor: creative labor, the labor of ordinariness, and celebrity lifestyle labor. This framework will be used throughout the rest of the book to analyze the extraordinarily ordinary celebrity as a marker of gendered, raced, and classed social identities. I argue *Us Weekly*'s main focus is on the private-side discourses that highlight celebrities as ordinary people and, crucially, uses this ordinariness to justify—or in some cases, challenge—their celebrity status. *Us Weekly* celebrates extraordinary celebrity lifestyles—the glamour of luxurious homes and vacations, designer clothes, and red carpet events—but at the same time insists that those living this life are ultimately just like us, thus using celebrity culture to reinforce the myth of meritocracy that suggests such lifestyles are available to any ordinary person who "works hard" and "deserves" them. Furthermore, the magazine's preoccupation with supposedly ordinary feminine concerns of intimate relationships, family, weddings, and fashion push its primarily female audience to identify with celebrities as markers of how to properly cultivate the feminine self within contemporary culture. This focus on ordinariness as a path to extraordinary status or as a marker of deserved extraordinary status is evident in the coverage of reality television celebrities within *Us Weekly*.

Chapter 2 centers on the labor of ordinariness and the ways in which the magazine harnesses the work of just being yourself to support the industrial goals of the magazine, the reality television program from which the celebrity emerges, and the celebrity herself. Drawing on examples from my *Us Weekly* archive, I argue that the magazine's existing focus on the private side of celebrity offers the necessary intertextuality that helps move the reality cast member out of the narrative boundaries of the reality television program and into celebrity culture, first as a celetoid and then, for a select few, as a more lasting extraordinarily ordinary celebrity. The magazine intensifies the reality star's claim to fame of just being herself by offering an extratextual venue through which to further negotiate the real self presented on the reality programs. This intertextuality presents a particular tension in construction of the reality celebrity image, as, rather than the traditional public/private split that shapes star images, the reality cast member is just being herself at all points. Thus, though both the reality program and the magazine claim to offer the real and authentic private self, this continued negotiation of the real individual and the ideological norms of identity she embodies emphasizes the right sort of performance of ordinariness as the core of the image. While celebrity culture is already a feminized space, this chapter traces the gendered nature of ordinariness within *Us Weekly* in which normative ideas about women's bodies, sexuality, maternal fitness, and overall value are reinforced through the celebrification of reality television cast members.

Using examples ranging from the early coverage of *Survivor* castaways to the cyclical coverage of the cast members of the Disney-owned *Bachelor/Bachelorette* franchise, this chapter identifies two key ways *Us Weekly*'s coverage of reality television cast members in the early twenty-first century works to "grow" celebrity from the ordinary individual through this negotiation: the production of reality celetoids tied to the promotion of the program and the construction of an extraordinarily ordinary celebrity grown by the magazine.

Though reality celebrities are famous for just being themselves, I argue in chapter 3 that the performance of the labor of ordinariness alone is not sufficient to transform the cast member into a celebrity; otherwise, any person who appeared in the media as themselves would become a celebrity. Ordinariness may help a cast member become a "media person" through appearance on the reality program, but to transition to the distinct category of "celebrity," the reality cast member must become something *more* than ordinary to merit this transition (Couldry, 2003, p. 107). She must become *extraordinary*, and *Us Weekly* is the vehicle where this extraordinariness is performed through celebrity lifestyle labor—appearing at red carpet events, doing promotional work, and living luxurious lifestyles—alongside traditional stars in ways that explicitly and implicitly frame reality cast members as part of the same celebrity world. Glossy celebrity weeklies like *Us Weekly* highlight the celebrity lifestyle labor of being yourself, but an extraordinary and "fabulous" self as the core of fame. This chapter explores celebrity lifestyle labor as a feminized form of work in which the star's primary attribute is the ability to attract public attention through her glamorous and consumption-based lifestyle and the ways in which this lifestyle fits within the magazine's commercial goals of appealing (and selling) to a primarily female audience. It delineates particular types of celebrity lifestyle labor as performed as reality cast members like Trista Sutter, Jenn Schefft, and the cast of *The Hills* move from reality cast member to reality celebrity, as well as a discussion of reality cast members, such as *Joe Millionaire's* Evan Marriott or Kate Gosselin from *Jon & Kate Plus 8*, whose failure to correctly perform celebrity lifestyle labor helps reinforce the hierarchy of celebrity culture and its attendant social norms. Such lifestyle labor is at the heart of contemporary celebrity culture, and reality celebrities make particularly potent symbols precisely because of their ordinary origins.

Ultimately, it is the blurring and blending of extraordinary and ordinary in *Us Weekly* that is essential to understanding the extraordinarily ordinary celebrity as a distinct form of celebrity. Whereas the previous chapters separated the forms of labor to study how they are deployed in the magazine around a range of reality cast members, chapter 4 offers a sustained analysis of *Us Weekly*'s involvement in transforming a single reality cast member, Lauren Conrad, from the MTV docuseries *The Hills*, into an extraordinarily ordinary celebrity. In this case study, I synthesize the arguments about the importance of the magazine's attention to both the labor of ordinariness and celebrity lifestyle labor as a means to grow the extraordinarily ordinary celebrity, as well as the industrial and social contexts that shaped this coverage. I argue that the construction of Conrad as a celebrity is inextricably tied to the coverage in the magazine, not simply her role on a reality television program, pointing to the importance of extratextual media like *Us Weekly* in the broader shift in celebrity culture around discourses of ordinariness.

The concluding chapter discusses the enduring legacy of the extraordinarily ordinary celebrity within contemporary celebrity and media cultures. Though print media continues to struggle, this chapter will point to *Us Weekly*'s continued relevance and place in contemporary popular culture, both as a continued leader in the print celebrity gossip market and, more broadly, as a foundational influence for the rise of DIY social media celebrity. It will explore how the continued centrality of the reality television celebrity to the formula of *Us Weekly* in the 2010s helped to maintain *Us Weekly*'s dominance in the gossip weekly market and build new cast members into celebrities. Moreover, it will detail important industrial shifts, particularly the sale of *Us Weekly* to American Media International (AMI), the publisher of the *National Enquirer*, in 2017 as part of a larger consolidation of the celebrity gossip market and the influence of AMI and its pro-Trump CEO David Pecker on the magazine's ideological aims. Second, it will recognize *Us Weekly*'s emphasis on ordinariness as a viable path to fame as a precursor to the ordinary fame produced on and through social media platforms like YouTube, Instagram, and Twitter. As celebrity culture continues to expand yet also continues to be dismissed as ephemeral and irrelevant, this book seeks to historicize and validate the important role of celebrity gossip in shaping everyday understandings of the self in contemporary culture.

CHAPTER 1

THE ORDINARY AND THE EXTRAORDINARY

UNPACKING THE CELEBRITY IMAGE

Appeals to ordinariness are a central ingredient in the alchemy of stardom, and entertainment news media and celebrity gossip weeklies—like *Us Weekly*—have long played a central role in the construction and circulation of this facet of the star image. Popular magazines, as Joshua Gamson (1992) argues, offer "implicit and explicit explanations . . . of why and how people become famous" (p. 2). As extratextual media sources outside of the space of public performance of talent or skill, this "why and how" is focused primarily on "the constant textual exposure of the 'real lives' of celebrities—in their most believable, 'ordinary' form" (p. 7). A key goal of this book is to understand how *Us Weekly* engaged this appeal to ordinariness in the early twenty-first century around the reality television cast member in ways that helped it shift the locus of fame toward the private and ordinary and, as a result, open space for the rise of the extraordinarily ordinary celebrity. This chapter unpacks the interplay between the ordinary and extraordinary in traditional analyses of celebrity to establish the particular parameters of the extraordinarily ordinary as a distinct form of celebrity. As will be made clear, my use of the term *extraordinarily ordinary* throughout this book centers on those stars whose fame originated from the performance of ordinariness on reality television programs in the early twenty-first century, even if their current status now eclipses those origins. The construction and circulation of the reality cast member as an extraordinarily ordinary celebrity in *Us Weekly* intensifies and extends these ordinary origins through appeals to feminized forms of celebrity labor. By unpacking these forms of labor and the ways in which they are used in *Us Weekly*'s coverage of reality television cast members, this book situates the extraordinarily ordinary celebrity as a significant symptom of the broader intensification of ordinariness and the private in the production of contemporary celebrity.

Celebrity and Labor

Emerging out of cinema studies and focused primarily on film stardom, Richard Dyer's (1986) theories of stardom provide a vital starting point for the consideration of contemporary celebrity and the conditions and forms of celebrity labor that produce celebrity images. His canonical work originates the premise that the star image is built on the juxtaposition of the public performing self and the private or "real" person behind that image. This intertextual image rests on an inherent tension between these public and private selves, balancing the extraordinary self—marked by the display of talent in public performances and the stage-managed glamour of celebrity lifestyles—with the ordinary and real self or the "irreducible core of being" that "remain[s] constant and give[s] sense to the person's actions and reactions" (p. 8). A star is not simply an image on a screen but is also a flesh-and-blood individual who exists in the real world. Though one side may come to dominate the image over the course of an individual's career, Dyer's view stakes a claim for the necessity of both the public-based performance and the revelation of the private self to the concept of the star and argues both of these selves are the result of labor on the part of the star (and her range of handlers). He contends that "stars are involved in making themselves into commodities; they are both labor and the thing that labor produces" (p. 5). In this view, stars are constructed or produced; they perform their images on-screen and in extratextual media, foregrounding narratives of labor and work in understanding the star image. The public performance is the more obvious, visible, and valued form of labor, with the labor of the private side remaining hidden to reinforce the authenticity or realness of the person behind the glamorous star facade and support her deserved fame. Thus, the public performance of talent or skill has long been understood as a, if not the, crucial component to most traditional conceptions of stardom.

However, Dyer's emphasis on intertextuality suggests, the mass media and in particular extratextual coverage of the private side of the star remain crucial to the star's social and economic power. Similarly, Robert Van Krieken (2012) points out that celebrity power is not simply a matter of talent but is tied more generally to the use of mass media as a means to attract attention. He claims that "layered on top of whatever talents, skills and moral virtues they may have—which is what constitutes their identity as a super-human football player, an incredibly beautiful and moving actress, or an aspiring singer—is their social function as larger or smaller bundles of attention capital, and this is what constitutes them as a celebrity" (p. 61). While the work of displaying one's talent has an obvious venue in films, pop songs, or athletic competitions, the celebrity also needs a place in which to circulate the private side of the image or to do the work of counterbalancing the extraordinary performing self with appeals to the ordinary and authentic private side. Van Krieken argues that early mass media technologies, particularly photography, that enabled the cheap and widespread distribution of images helped to incorporate celebrities into everyday life as their real, rather than their performing, selves. Photographic images of celebrities, from the early *carte-de-visites* of the mid-nineteenth century to the paparazzi snaps that currently populate gossip media, brought celebrities closer to audiences by giving the public the ability to "see what a celebrity *really* looked like" (p. 41, emphasis in original). As a result, a wide array of extratextual mass media forms, including entertainment news media and gossip magazines, emerged as the vehicle through which the celebrity does the work of performing her real self as a means to shore up the attention to the public image. This performance of the private and ordinary self outside of the public performance thus became a necessary means to generate and *regenerate* the attention capital that supports the social and economic power of celebrities. Unlike the more obvious work of "doing something" to enter the public eye, however, this work of "just being yourself" in these extratextual sources is hidden beneath claims of authenticity and ordinariness, at once humanizing the celebrities and intensifying their roles as markers of identity within contemporary culture.

To understand the reality television celebrity's intervention into this traditional view of celebrity, this book expands on these underlying notions of labor that shape the production and circulation of celebrity images. I begin by expanding the prevailing discussion of celebrity labor by delineating three distinct yet overlapping forms: creative labor, the labor of ordinariness, and celebrity lifestyle labor. How these forms of labor are specifically deployed in *Us Weekly*'s coverage of reality television cast members in the early 2000s will be explored in more detail in subsequent chapters, but I here sketch a basic definition of each form. Broadly, I argue that while all these forms of labor are necessary to the production and circulation of any celebrity image, including traditional stars, understanding each as a separate form helps to illuminate the complex parameters of celebrity and, more crucially for this project, to recognize the particular intersections that produce the reality television celebrity as extraordinarily ordinary. The performance of these various forms may contribute to celebrity but in no way guarantees it. As with all forms of celebrity, the extraordinarily ordinary celebrity is hierarchical, with those who more successfully perform certain forms of labor rising to the top and building a lasting fame while others find only short-lived or celetoid-level success. Moreover, expanding the forms of celebrity labor also lays bare the cultural contexts that shape the identities produced through such labor and the ways in which they circulate in culture. The work of just being yourself shapes and is shaped by cultural norms of gender, race, class, and sexuality, with only the "right" kind of self emerging as a top extraordinarily ordinary celebrity. The notions of deserving fame versus being famous for being famous that are at the core of reality television celebrity are wrapped up in gendered notions of the kind of labor performed in the service of stardom. Even as the extraordinarily ordinary celebrity helps intensify the importance of ordinariness to celebrity culture, it is also frequently denigrated as a lesser form of fame because of the dominance of the more hidden and feminized forms of labor associated with performance of the private and ordinary self.

Creative Labor

It has never been the case that talent alone makes a star. The notion of talent itself is, as Dyer (1979/1998) points out, historically and culturally specific and, more importantly, subjective. He says, "Not all highly talented performers become stars, nor are all stars highly talented" (p. 16). But traditional stars claim to *do* something to merit at least the initial attention of the public. Richard deCordova (1991) calls this "creative labor" and suggests it is the means through which the star's work on stage or screen is framed as fictional or at least intentionally performative and, therefore, separate from the real individual who does this work (p. 21). For example, while some might question Britney Spears's claim to talent, she nevertheless entered the realm of celebrity through her performances as a pop singer. Spears retains some claim to traditional celebrity through her continued creative labor as a pop star (e.g., releasing albums and performing publicly). Such claims have arguably been eclipsed by the focus on the trials and tribulations of her private life within extratextual media, refocusing the core of her image on her private self. But this remains consistent with Dyer's original intertextual formulation of stardom, as the private-side discourses counterbalance and ultimately serve to draw audiences back to the creative labor that initiated her presence within celebrity culture.

In the hierarchy of celebrity, those at the top (the A-list celebrities) are typically closely tied to, if not lauded for, their creative labor, prioritizing this work as the reason for fame. A star like Meryl Streep or Kate Winslet earned and maintains her fame through celebrated acting performances. Christine Geraghty (2000) labels these stars as "performers" whose images are "defined by work and are often associated with the high cultural values of theatrical performance, even when that performance takes place in film or television" (p. 188). Access to these women's private life does exist in entertainment and, to a lesser extent, gossip media, but the core of the image remains rooted in the "good work" of the public performance. Even those A-listers whose private lives are on greater display in extratextual media, particularly in relation to scandals, can still retain their top position through appeals to creative labor. Consider stars like Elizabeth Taylor or Angelina Jolie, whose personal lives have been fodder for tabloid gossip. Yet, unlike Britney Spears, these performers' creative work remains more centrally important to the image because the work is framed as good and thus their fame deserved. Spears, dogged throughout her career with claims of lip-syncing and denigrated for her association with the lesser cultural form of pop music, lacks the good creative labor of someone like Taylor or Jolie, whose Oscar-nominated roles and appearances in "quality" cinema shore up the image as a deserved star despite the presence of any private-life scandal. Nevertheless, Spears is not a purely private-side-focused star, as her songs and performances—her creative labor—continue to maintain an important place in her overall image.

In contrast, the reality celebrity would appear to be excluded from this sort of labor, as the rhetoric of reality television suggests these individuals are *not* performing for the cameras and have no such counterbalance to offer audiences. This is not to suggest the reality television program plays no role in the image of the reality television celebrity. It does provide an initial text in which the public image is constructed and circulated and, as will be clear in the case studies in the chapters that follow, is used as a way to measure the authenticity of the image. But the labor performed in this space is not generally assumed to be the creative labor of public performance and does not work as a space of intertextuality in the same way because it is assumed to be simply another point of access to the private and real self. Thus, in order to make sense of their increased presence in celebrity culture and the impact of these extraordinarily ordinary celebrities on contemporary notions of fame, I want to highlight the importance of two more feminized and thereby less visible forms of work—the labor of ordinariness and celebrity lifestyle labor—and the spaces in which they are performed to the construction of the reality television celebrity image.

The Labor of Ordinariness

In traditional conceptions of stardom, the labor of ordinariness is framed as the opposite of creative labor, separating the display of the (allegedly) natural and authentic self from the conscious construction of the creative performance. It is performed outside of but typically in service to the media text in which creative labor is performed, distancing this work from that more intentionally performative space and allowing the audience to feel a more intimate connection to the extraordinary individual admired on stage or screen. Julie Wilson (2014) claims: "On-screen stars play characters that often embody social types (e.g., the girl next door or the femme fatale), while off screen, in magazines and on popular talk shows, they appear as 'real' people who, like their audiences, experience the highs and lows of life, wrestling with issues to do with family, love, and work" (p. 423). While the labor of ordinariness has always been key to the construction of the star as an intertextual image, scholarship has also offered a crucial reexamination of the role of the private to the celebrity image (Gamson, 1994, 2011; Geraghty, 2000; Holmes, 2004a, 2005; Meyers, 2013; Redmond, 2014; Turner, 2004, 2010). Broadly, these scholars argue the increased public attention to the private and ordinary self reconfigures Dyer's original notions of stardom toward the more contemporary category of celebrity by essentially eliminating not only "the distinction between deserving and underserving people" but also the need to engage in creative labor to earn fame (Gamson, 1994, p. 10). Such a shift opens the category of celebrity to the ordinary individual by tying fame to attention capital, by whatever means, over talent.

Graeme Turner (2004) contends the "precise moment a public figure becomes a celebrity" can be traced to the moment when reporting about the public figure is eclipsed by a focus on his or her private life (p. 8). While the creative labor is more obvious or visible in the construction of the image, the private self on offer in celebrity magazines is no less a construction or result of labor on the part of the celebrity and her handlers. However, these sources work to obscure the existence of this *as labor* to preserve the appeal to the authentic and real image offered to audiences. A magazine interview with a celebrity, for example, shows the star at home or speaking "off the cuff" about her family or daily life but is often the result of a carefully negotiated list of questions and/or controlled answers on the part of the celebrity. A fundamental part of revealing the private self is appearing as if no labor is being performed at all and that the star is just being herself. This promotes what Sue Collins (2008) calls the "intertextual capital" of the celebrity commodity, allowing audiences to stitch together a coherent image drawn from both the extraordinary performing self and the private and ordinary self. To acquire high intertextual capital, traditional celebrities must appear unstaged in their private lives, maintaining the illusion that their work and the attention capital gained from performing that work remain tied to the performing self. Here, the gendered nature of the celebrity hierarchy begins to emerge. True and deserved fame is valorized as a public and masculinized form of consciously produced labor (e.g., the creative labor discussed above) in contrast to the more private, feminized, and often invisible labor of ordinariness. Geraghty (2000) points out that the distinction between "star" and "celebrity" is a feminized one that devalues "celebrities" because of their tie to the feminine. She contends, "Women function effectively as spectacle in the press and on television as well as in the cinema. In addition, the common association in popular culture between women and the private sphere of personal relationships and domesticity fits with the emphasis, in the discourse of celebrity, on the private life and leisure activity of the star" (p. 196). Much of the social critique of celebrity is rooted in a dismissal of the forms of private and ordinary labor of just being oneself that underscore the celebrity on offer in spaces like celebrity gossip media. When these once hidden feminine labors and concerns are made visible as part of the construction of fame, the individual who performs these labors is maligned as a "mere celebrity" and/or assumed to be "famous for doing nothing."

Concern about the role of private-side discourses is not a new one, as evidenced by Daniel Boorstin's (1964) oft-quoted lament that "the machinery of information" has shifted our attention from "the person known for some serious achievement" to the "new-fashioned celebrity . . . whose main characteristic is his well-knowness" (pp. 59–60). While Boorstin's pessimistic view positions celebrity as a site of false meaning and media manufacture, his point about the increased media attention to celebrities and, more crucially, the specific emphasis of this coverage on the private self exposes an important shift in the role of the extratextual sources to the construction and maintenance of modern fame that anticipates the rise of reality television celebrity. At the same time, his negative view reveals a deeper and abiding patriarchal concern about celebrity culture as a destructive social force that denigrates the work of true greatness or talent by elevating the concerns and labors of the private sphere into the public purview. He says, "Our emphasis on their marital relations and sexual habits, on their tastes in smoking, drinking, dress, sports cars, and interior decoration is our desperate effort to distinguish among the indistinguishable" (p. 65). Boorstin reasserts a binary masculine/feminine split in which only those individualist acts of achievement in the public sphere are truly worthy of the status of the "hero" or the "great man." To be a great man, one must actually work—or perform *publicly visible* work—to achieve it, thus diminishing the feminine concerns and labors of the private sphere as outside of greatness and the celebrities who embody them as inauthentic and undeserving of fame. This distinction between the masculine public sphere of talent and achievement and the feminine private sphere of ordinariness continues to shape contemporary notions of celebrity, as seen in the popular dismissal of the reality television celebrity. Viewing reality stars as famous for being famous is about the grounding of the image in the private and real self rather than on the working self made visible through creative labor.

Echoing Boorstin, Chris Rojek (2001) argues that the expansion of the mass media has resulted in the rise of "attributed celebrities" who are "famous for being famous," riding the wave of concentrated media attention to his or her private life rather than talent to celebrity status (p. 18). The attributed celebrity stands in contrast to the "achieved celebrity," whose fame at least initially rests on a claim to talent—however dubious—and for performing that talent in the public eye (ibid.). Following the Dyer model, the achieved celebrity does not necessarily have to be *good* at that talent but must have a public persona that rests on a performing self that is necessarily distinct from the private self. For Rojek, the centrality of the private self to celebrity within contemporary media culture has also opened space for a more "compressed, concentrated" form of the attributed celebrity in which media attention to the private and ordinary self precedes any potential talent-based claims (p. 20). These are individuals who use attention to the private self, not any claim to talent or skill, as the point of entry into the public eye. Rojek (2001) calls these "celetoids" and argues they are "the accessories of cultures organized around mass communications and staged authenticity . . . who command media attention one day and are forgotten the next" (pp. 20–21). In other words, the celetoid is evidence of a celebrity culture marked by the attention-generating power of the labor of ordinariness rather than doing the "real" work of creative labor.

The reality star would seem to be an obvious contemporary example of the celetoid, whose place in the public eye relies primarily on media attention to the private self at all points. Julie A. Wilson (2014) points out that the coverage of reality celebrities in such gossip weeklies as *Us Weekly* "do[es] not primarily work to construct a broader star image," as it does for traditional stars (p. 247). Instead, such coverage "figure[s] as direct extensions of reality formats, as they publicize and comment on events that have already aired or anticipate and preview 'real' happenings to come" (ibid.). This makes the reality star distinct from the traditional star because her celebrity is born from the subsuming of creative labor into the labor of ordinariness. Put differently, reality celebrities are dismissed as famous for "doing nothing" because their images are based on the performance of invisible and feminized forms of celebrity labor and, importantly, do not include the counterbalance of the more masculinized consciously performative creative labor. But the rise of reality television celebrity calls for a further expansion of the role of labor that recognizes what these sorts of celebrities actually *do* in the service of building their celebrity, the spaces in which they do this work, and the ways in which such labor helps maintain the broader social power of celebrities. As will be discussed in more detail in chapter 2, more than simply famous for being famous, I argue, the various forms of extraordinarily ordinary celebrity can be more accurately described as those famous for just being themselves. For these celebrities, the public display of talent—the traditional site of celebrity labor—is subordinated to a different sort of labor: the feminized work of performing the ordinary self within celebrity culture and the performance of such labor within the extratextual gossip press.

Celebrity Lifestyle Labor

Just as talent alone cannot produce fame, neither can the performance of the labor of ordinariness within popular media alone provide the basis for celebrity status; otherwise, anyone visible in the media for any reason would be considered a celebrity. Reality cast members thus require celebrification, or intertextual capital that counterbalances the ordinary self and positions them as extraordinary. They must enter the realm of celebrity culture by being elevated away from ordinariness (while still maintaining a tie to it). Lacking the creative labor to support traditional appeals to extraordinariness, the key to celebrification for reality cast members instead rests on a third category of labor that bridges the other two forms to create a category I call celebrity lifestyle labor. This is not the work of *doing* but rather the work of *being* a celebrity, a known property whose extraordinary self can be trotted out for publicity and attention that benefits both the individual image and the industrial forces behind it. Such labor includes promotional work, like appearing on talk shows, attending film premieres, or doing magazine interviews, as well as simply living the celebrity life by engaging in conspicuous consumption—wearing designer clothes, taking lavish vacations, or frequenting glamorous nightclubs. This labor is performed primarily in extratextual media, as it is not simply living this lifestyle but *visibly* and *publicly* living this lifestyle that helps elevate one to the status of celebrity. Celebrity lifestyle labor rests on the revelation of the real or private self, as the star here is not meant to be performing in the same way she does in the creative labor role but in ways that highlight the pizzazz, glamour, and extraordinariness of that ordinary (celebrity) self.

Indeed, much of the celebrity gossip media exists primarily, if not exclusively, to show stars living a celebrity lifestyle rather than to explicitly discuss their creative projects. *Us Weekly*, for example, features only a few film or music reviews (offering only short blurbs about new films, television programs, or albums at the back of the issue) and pays little attention to box office reports, project development news, or other industry analysis. The magazine often discusses stars with no reference to projects, assuming the reader already knows who they are and keeping the focus on the private-side details. For example, a short story about Cameron Diaz dating Bradley Cooper in the October 15, 2007, issue never once mentioned any projects for either actor and instead centered on where the couple had been spotted and how "cute" they are together (Cameron Diaz's new romance, p. 45). When a star's upcoming project is mentioned, it is generally only to orient the reader to the star's place in popular culture. For example, a photo feature in the October 15, 2007, issue called "Celeb Snaps!" featured multiple "candid" photos from "the *Us* photo booth" at the magazine's annual Hot Hollywood party. The captions briefly mentioned the projects of some stars to remind us who they are, but the focus was clearly on the real self captured enjoying the event. The main photo featured *Heroes* stars Greg Grunberg and Adrian Pasdar talking about the event as their "guys' night" as "[their] wives are with the kids" rather than any discussion of their popular television show (p. 34). Similarly, captions for the four offset photos included: "KELIS (right) posed with *Heroes*' DANIA RAMIREZ," "Former *Nip/Tuck* star SANAA LATHAN looked elegant in a deep V," "'I wanted a change,' TARYN MANNING says of her darker hair," and "EMILY PROCTOR (left) chatted up *CSI* costar EVA LA RUE" (ibid.). These captions provide some intertextuality to the image by reminding the reader of the celebrity's creative labor, but it is brief and subordinated to the emphasis on the lifestyle labor—here demonstrated through the dominance of the photos of the stars appearing as themselves at a Hollywood event in fabulous clothes and with beautiful hair and not talking about their projects.

Celebrity lifestyle labor, like the labor of ordinariness, draws on the idea that the display of the private is itself a form of work but a feminized one that is most effective when it appears not to be work. As will be evident in the discussion of *Us Weekly*'s coverage of reality cast members' performance of this labor, it is the work of performing (but not appearing to consciously construct) the right sort of gendered (and classed and raced) ordinary self that helps elevate that cast member into the extraordinary realm of celebrity culture by living it in its most idealized form. In this example, all the stars are framed in feminized ways, either through relationships (Grunberg and Pasdar's "guys night" or Proctor and La Rue "chatting") or through a tie to beauty and fashion (Lathan's "elegant" outfit and Manning's "darker hair"), with the attention to their creative work as secondary, if mentioned at all. That half of the stars featured in this one-page photo spread are women of color is notable in a magazine that, as with celebrity culture more broadly, overwhelmingly focuses on white celebrities. However, such inclusion of women of color is part of the magazine's narrative of celebrity as a postracial meritocracy in which color does not matter and anyone can rise to the top through the successful performance of the self. Such postracial logics, as will be discussed later in this book, are what Kristen Warner (2017) calls "plastic representation" in which the mere visibility of difference serves "to flatten the expectation to desire anything more," offering pleasure in seeing diverse representation without truly engaging with the ways in which race, gender, and sexuality operate within celebrity culture (para. 14). In *Us Weekly*, the presence of celebrities of color as part of the glamorous world of celebrity reinforces the myth of meritocracy that suggests anyone can become famous, but such representation lacks any interrogation of the ways in which the labor of ordinariness and celebrity lifestyle labor overwhelmingly centers whiteness as the norm by which all celebrities are judged and the lack of access and choices people of color, particularly women of color, have in successfully performing such labor.

Celebrity lifestyle labor is about the ways in which celebrities live as both evidence of and the result of their fame. It is the form that most convincingly blurs the distinctions between extraordinary and ordinary, focusing on the way a seemingly innate specialness elevates the individual into an extraordinary lifestyle. In this way, celebrity lifestyle labor is divorced from creative labor while still standing in as evidence of deserved success that (presumably) results from such labor. In *Us Weekly*, celebrities are shown to live glamorous lives that are unlike the average person's because they are unlike the average person. They are "the most something-or-other in the world—the most beautiful, the most expensive, the most sexy" (Dyer, 1998, p. 43). They drive expensive cars, wear expensive clothes, go to exclusive parties, and, importantly, are shown in moments of leisure (getting coffee, at the beach, going shopping), not moments of work. Though an appeal to the ordinary self continues to matter, this is the space of celebrification, in which the real person gets to live the lavish life that demonstrates celebrity status. This is not unique to reality stars, as celebrity lifestyle labor is central to the work of traditional celebrities as well. However, this form of labor, which will be discussed in more detail in chapter three, is particularly crucial to the celebrification of reality cast members because it provides the intertextual capital or the means of elevating their performance of ordinariness into the extraordinary realm of celebrity culture. That is, living the right kind of celebrity lifestyle (or, alternatively, being a cautionary tale of how *not* to live) functions as a form of attention capital that attracts gossip media coverage. Of course, such coverage itself then generates even more attention, reproducing and intensifying the celebrity of the once ordinary individual. I argue the extratextual gossip press, and specifically *Us Weekly*, is a central vehicle for the production and circulation of reality cast members as celebrities by offering a space for the individual to perform both the labor of ordinariness (intensifying her work on the reality show as "herself") and celebrity lifestyle labor, thus producing an extraordinarily ordinary celebrity.

Reality Television Celebrity as Extraordinarily Ordinary

The exploration of the tensions between the private/ordinary and public/extraordinary sides of the celebrity image is foundational to the study of celebrity culture, and indeed the term *extraordinarily ordinary* has previously been used to delineate a category of celebrity arising from reality television. Derek Kompare (2004) points to *The Osbournes*—the "first reality sitcom," centered on the domestic life of the heavy metal star Ozzy Osbourne and his raucous family—and the advent of "celebreality" in the early 2000s as a moment of rupture within celebrity culture that explicitly constructs a new extraordinarily ordinary celebrity. He says, "The point of *The Osbournes* is to distinguish the 'real' Ozzy (and his family) from that already-established celebrity. Accordingly, the series pushes Ozzy's star persona to the background. . . . Instead, we are constantly shown a 'backstage' Ozzy, one closer to the established codes of sitcom representation: somewhat addled, middle-aged dad who just happens to be a rock star" (p. 110). Following in the tradition of the more controlled celebrity media profile, in which the star (and her handlers) exchange control over the representation of the image for deeper access to the star's private life, celebreality promises a real and authentic look at the lives of established celebrities. The celebreality show is a vehicle for the star's (controlled) performance of the labor of ordinariness, but it rests on the notion that he or she is *already* famous in a more traditional sense (e.g., with a grounding in a claim to the public performance of a talent or skill). The star's fame may have faded, and indeed the D-List celetoid is a mainstay of the celebreality subgenre (see *The Surreal Life* [2003–2006], *Hogan Knows Best* [2005–2007], *Being Bobby Brown* [2005], *Kathy Griffin: My Life on the D-List* [2005–2010], *Flavor of Love* [2006–2008], and *Celebrity Big Brother* [2008–present], to name a few), but at least traces remain to justify the public attention to the star's private life on the show.

It is neither the case that simply being on a reality television program or being covered in *Us Weekly* alone makes one extraordinarily ordinary in the sense in which I am engaging the term. Instead, I argue it is about the intertextuality or the performance of labor across these forms that is important to understanding this category. As Kompare's example of Ozzy Osbourne illustrates, many existing achieved celebrities have sought to use the exposure of the private self on reality television as a way to reclaim celebrity status or to regain control over a damaged celebrity image, which leads to coverage in the magazine. MTV's *Newlyweds: Nick & Jessica* (2003–2005), for example, was a typical celebreality program that offered a glimpse of the real lives of pop stars Jessica Simpson and Nick Lachey during the early years of their marriage, helping to launch these middling pop singers into a greater level of celebrity through the public display of their private selves. It was effective in generating attention capital that transferred to (and was also increased by) coverage in the gossip media, as the couple's relationship and eventual divorce was featured heavily in *Us Weekly* during the mid-2000s. However, these are celebrities who used reality television as an outlet *for* their existing images rather than celebrities who were made *by* reality television. Thus, Jessica Simpson / Nick Lachey and Ozzy Osbourne represent the sort of extraordinarily ordinary celebrities set out by Kompare that rely on existing fame via creative labor as a starting point. That is, I argue, they were extraordinary *before* they were ordinary, and thus their pre-existing fame places them outside the scope of this project. In contrast, as will be explored throughout this book, the increased attention in *Us Weekly* to reality television celebrities who have no prior claim to fame and typically no creative labor in which to ground such a claim suggests the extraordinarily ordinary celebrity may also be produced in the opposite way from Kompare's original formulation—from ordinary to extraordinary.

The production of the extraordinarily ordinary celebrity points to the slipperiness of this term and the complexity of celebrity culture's hierarchical system. I am interested in the ways in which *Us Weekly* foments attention capital for particular individuals by elevating the ordinary self already on offer in the reality television program through an appeal to both the labor of ordinariness and celebrity lifestyle labor. For example, Kim Kardashian, who is perhaps the quintessential celetoid of contemporary celebrity culture, provides an example of the complexity of the category of extraordinarily ordinary reality celebrity. As Alice Leppert (2015) suggests, Kim and her family "have come to occupy a liminal space of reality celebrity—between ordinary fame-seekers and 'real' celebrities showing that they're 'just like us'" (p. 216). This liminality, born of the symbiotic relationship between reality television and gossip media in the fame cycle of a celebrity, has helped elevate Kim to the form of extraordinarily ordinary celebrity she inhabits today (Deller, 2016). While she had no prior claim to talent or skill to ground her image in creative labor, some may argue that Kim was not completely unknown within celebrity culture prior to her appearance on *Keeping Up with the Kardashians* (*KUWTK*, 2007–present). She experienced at least a celetoid level of attributed fame by virtue of her friendship with Paris Hilton, her sex tape with the R & B star Ray-J, and the fact that her father, Robert Kardashian, was famous as one of the defense attorneys in the O. J. Simpson murder trial. However, in a reversal of the representation of Ozzy Osbourne's backstage life on *The Osbournes*, *KUWTK* highlights Kim's (and her family's) labor as a celebrity without offering any creative labor justification for *why* she is famous. Leppert (2015) claims the show "has always narrativized fame-work, with its pilot episode revolving around Kim debating how much to reveal about her sex tape in her first television interview with Tyra Banks and the second episode focusing on Kris struggling to manage all of Kim's work commitments" (p. 219). Unlike other reality shows that hide the celebrity lifestyle labor of its ordinary cast members, as will be made clear in my discussion of *The Hills* in chapter 4, *KUWTK* explicitly depicts Kim doing the work of *being* a celebrity and, crucially, the impact of that labor on her personal life. The show highlights Kim just being herself and reminds viewers through the appeals to celebrity lifestyle labor that she is worthy of celebrity status. In other words, it combines the celebrity lifestyle labor and the labor of ordinariness that support the construction of the extraordinarily ordinary celebrity, rooting her image in the public display of the private self not in creative labor.

The combination of celebrity lifestyle labor and the labor of ordinariness that constructs Kim's image on *KUWTK* mirrors the subsequent coverage of her in *Us Weekly*, thus further justifying my attention to her. The reality program remains central to her image, as it was only after *KUWTK* premiered that she began to appear more regularly in *Us Weekly*. Kim's first appearance in *Us Weekly* was in a paparazzi photo alongside Paris Hilton[1] in the January 22, 2007, issue (Cina, 2007, pp. 68–69). Here, Kim was a hanger-on—celebrity adjacent but not someone who matched Paris's attention-getting capacity and pre-existing extraordinariness. She did not reappear again until she was included in a "Who Wore It Best" photo feature on July 2, just as E! was beginning to promote the fall premiere of *KUWTK*, a clear appeal to her celebrity lifestyle labor without any obvious connection to creative labor behind that celebrity (McColgin, 2007, p. 6). She began regularly appearing in 2008 after the show became a success, and she, along with her sisters, Kourtney and Khloé, and her mother, Kris (and later younger half sisters, Kendall and Kylie Jenner), became regular fixtures of celebrity weeklies and E! reality programming in the 2010s. While Kim's contemporary fame has far exceeded that of most other extraordinarily ordinary reality television celebrities, her image nevertheless originated in and continues to be constructed through the labor of ordinariness (albeit often in the midst of celebrity lifestyle labor) on the show itself, as well as the subsequent media attention to her celebrity lifestyle labor. Her rise to fame had only just begun during the time frame covered by this project, but Kim's image illustrates the ways in which the forms of labor producing celebrity and the venues where such labor is performed have shifted in contemporary celebrity culture. As will be explored throughout this book, a symbiotic relationship exists between reality television and gossip media as venues for the performance of the labor of ordinariness and celebrity lifestyle labor necessary to construct the extraordinarily ordinary celebrity. Neither is solely responsible for the elevation of reality cast members to celebrity status, but understanding the role each plays sheds light on the intensification of the ordinary within celebrity culture.

Reality TV and Ordinariness

Despite the need for intertextuality, the reality program maintains a key place within the reality television celebrity's image, as it is both the site of the original public performance—where they *do* something within the public eye—and simultaneously a place where audiences discover the individual as a real and ordinary person. Mark Andrejevic (2002) argues the camera's "perpetual surveillance" of the daily lives of a reality program's cast members acts as "the antidote to artificial interactions," allowing audiences to believe that despite any control "producers have in the editing process," reality TV ultimately presents "real" people who are just "being themselves" (p. 261). While not the same as creative labor, as these stars are not supposed to be "performing," it is the site of the front-stage or performed self that is tied to the work of being on television. It is a space in which the publicly visible labor of being a "media person" is connected to the more invisible labor of ordinariness in ways that highlight the "real" and "authentic" self as the core of the image (Couldry, 2003). Thus, reality television is self-consciously focused on the labor of ordinariness, even as it hides the fact that this is itself a form of work.

Annette Hill (2005) defines reality television as "a catch-all category that includes a wide range of entertainment programmes about real people" (p. 2). Indeed, the contemporary media landscape has taken what Turner (2004) calls a "demotic turn," in which "ordinary people have never been more visible" across media discourses (p. 83). This has important implications for celebrity, as the growth of media genres focused on the ordinary individual, particularly reality television and its myriad subgenres, has intensified both the "demand for ordinary people desiring 'celebrification'" and the centrality of discourses of ordinariness to celebrity culture (Turner, 2010, p. 13). The demotic turn enables media industries to produce and circulate celebrities "on a much larger scale than ever before" not through a focus on talent or achieved claims to fame but instead on the performance of the labor of ordinariness within the confines of various reality television formats (ibid.). This would appear, on the surface, to offer greater cultural value to the invisible forms of feminized work that underscores the labor of ordinariness. However, as Turner (2004) emphasizes, the demotic turn is not a democratic one in which media discourses diversify and a greater range of voices are brought into the public sphere. Rather, he argues, "what motivates the media's mining of the ordinary seems to be its capacity to generate the performance of endless and unmotivated diversity for its own sake. . . . It is important to remember that celebrity remains a hierarchical and exclusive phenomenon, no matter how much it proliferates. It is in the interests of those who operate this hierarchy in the contemporary context, however, to disavow its exclusivity; maybe what we are watching in the demotic turn is the celebrity industries' improved capacity to do this through the media" (p. 83). The greater opportunity for ordinary individuals to appear on television because of the rise of reality programming disguises the ways in which what is represented as "ordinary" is "an illusion of normality" that ultimately re-inscribes hegemonic ideologies about the self (Bonner, 2003, p. 32; Grindstaff, 2014). Reality television and celebrity culture both work to reify the right kind of identity and denigrate those who fall outside those narrow boundaries, thus reaffirming the ideological confines of identity that shape the extraordinarily ordinary celebrity.

Similarly, Laura Grindstaff (2011) sees reality television as a form of "'self-service television' in which producers construct the necessary conditions of performance and real-people serve themselves (more or less successfully) to these performances" (p. 44). This obscures the very manufacture of this ordinariness by the media producers, inserting ordinary people into the realm of celebrity in ways consistent with normative ideologies about gender, race, sexuality, and class. Celebrity culture's hierarchical system suggests celebrities are special individuals, but the rise of the reality star turns audiences away from talent as the reason for our attention to a "special" individual and toward the performance of the "right" sort of ordinary self. Grindstaff (2011) says, "Ordinary celebrity marks the individual as special but not categorically 'outside' or 'beyond' the everyday"; thus the identities she embodies seem more attainable and identifiable to the audience, even as they reflect the same normative ideologies attached to traditional stars (p. 54). The hierarchy of celebrity is also reinforced by the fact that not all ordinary people on television become celebrities, thus demanding a closer look at the reality celebrity to see which sorts of ordinary identities are brought into the field of celebrity and how such extratextual sources as *Us Weekly* work to make such ordinariness extraordinary.

The docusoap subgenre of reality television, in particular, makes the labor of ordinariness central to the public persona of its cast members in ways that closely align with the private discourses of celebrity weeklies and the attendant feminized work of the private sphere. This subgenre attempts to document social realities as they unfold by following "a chosen set of 'real life' people . . . for a period of time as they went about whatever was the focus of the camera's attention" (Bonner, 2003, p. 25). As their name suggests, these "real-life" soap operas track the domestic and personal lives of the cast members, focusing on intimate relationships and domestic spaces. These character-driven dramas are further marked by cast members "indulging in gossipy, soap-like forms of interchange" as a means to drive the narrative (Kilborn, 2003, p. 82). The narrative events may be framed as the ordinary and everyday lives of cast members, such as *The Hills* purporting to document the lives of a group of twenty-something friends in Los Angeles or *Jon and Kate Plus 8* documenting the daily lives of a family with eight children. Or they may be somewhat more contrived in setting to capture "real" reactions, such as *The Bachelor/Bachelorette*'s game-doc premise of a dating competition or *The Real World*'s social experiment format of producer-assembled groups of twenty-something strangers made to live together to see "what happens when people stop being polite and start getting real."

Annette Hill (2015) points out the docusoap "is often deeply banal" because of its focus on the ordinary events of the daily lives of cast members, yet it is through this banality that the cast members' real selves are alleged to emerge (p. 8). Not only do audiences see the story lines unfolding naturally within the daily lives of cast members; the cast members are often called on to comment on the action either through voice-overs or confessional-style direct address cutaways in ways that purport to offer a deeper truth about those events. The narrative techniques of the docusoap, according to Susan Murray and Laurie Ouellette (2004), promise audiences "revelatory insight into the lives of others as it withholds and subverts full access to it" (p. 6). In contrast to talent or skill-based competitions like *American Idol* or *Project Runway*, which certainly include docusoap aspects on top of the contest format, the range of docusoap programs are united by the notion that the cast members are simply performing as themselves for the cameras, thus offering up the private self for public consumption. That the cast members of some of the decade's most popular and enduring franchises, including ABC's *The Bachelor/Bachelorette* (2002–present), MTV's *Laguna Beach* (2004–2006) and *The Hills* (2006–2010), and Bravo's *Real Housewives* series (beginning with *Real Housewives of Orange County* in 2006 and continuing with eight additional spin-offs), are overwhelmingly female is no coincidence, as the emphasis on the domestic and emotional lives of the cast members makes the docusoap a highly feminized space. Thus, celebrities that emerge from this genre are already steeped in discourses of the ordinary and the real, offering an image through which audiences are invited to negotiate norms of femininity in everyday life.

Unlike achieved celebrities who possess a talent that is presumably transferable to other texts (e.g., an actress can make more films), the private-side focus of reality television seems to suggest reality celebrity has nothing else to offer but the ordinary self already available within the program's narrative (Turner, 2004). In fact, the continued emphasis on these individuals as ordinary within the narrative of the show depends on them remaining just like us, to the extent that any celebrification of the individual outside of the show is often hidden, as will be discussed in chapter 4's case study of Lauren Conrad. A more typical reality cast member may, at best, be transferrable to other reality programs, and some reality stars do extend their time in the public eye by jumping from franchise to franchise. For example, MTV's *The Challenge* (1998–present, originally titled *Road Rules: All Stars* and then *Real World/Road Rules Challenge*) pits cast members from several of the network's other reality programs, including *The Real World*, *Road Rules*, and *Are You the One?*, against each other in a competition-style reality program. These individuals continue to perform their real selves within the confines of reality programming and have little purchase outside of it. Certainly this is an extension of what Sue Collins (2008) calls the "dispensable celebrity" that "operates out of an expanded field of labor stock to include nonunion low-cost workers," to "shelters the larger system of celebrity valorization from the dual problems of scarcity and clutter" (p. 90). Reality cast members are stars here inasmuch as they are known commodities to be shuffled around, cashing in their small amount of attention capital to draw viewers to the new programs. Yet other reality cast members, such as those discussed throughout this book, are not quite as dispensable, because of an increased intertextuality brought about through coverage in extratextual sources like *Us Weekly*. For example, after first finding fame as the villains on *The Hills*, Spencer Pratt and Heidi Montag[2] appeared as themselves on the second season of the U.S. version of *I'm a Celebrity . . . Get Me out of Here* (2009), two seasons of the British version of *Celebrity Big Brother* (2009 and 2013), and one season of *Marriage Boot Camp* (2015). But unlike the more interchangeable *Challenge* stars, the durability of their celebrity is a result of the extratextual media attention to them outside of (though in ways related to) the selves on offer in the reality programs. As with the other reality celebrities explored throughout this book, Spencer's and Heidi's fame points to deeper symbiotic industrial and cultural relationships between reality television and gossip media in the production and circulation of the extraordinarily ordinary celebrity. But it also points to the hierarchical nature of extraordinarily ordinary celebrity, which encompasses a range of reality celebrity statuses and gives greater cultural power to those who properly uphold normative ideologies of identity while keeping others, like Spencer and Heidi, around as cautionary tales of how *not* to be.

Celebrity Media and Ordinariness

Misha Kavka (2012) claims, "Reality television now self-consciously functions as part of the celebrity-making apparatus, interacting with other media forms and entertainment industries to produce and promote fame" (p. 146). The celebrification of reality television cast members, as with traditional stars, could not happen without the efforts of the extratextual celebrity media. The entertainment-news media, and particularly the celebrity weeklies, are fundamental spaces for the reality television celebrity because they are primarily concerned with the private self of the star, offering a space of intertextuality in which the reality cast member can perform the labor of ordinariness outside of the reality television program. These magazines bring us behind the mask of the public persona to see the real person in his or her private life. Yet this private and ordinary self is still offered up for public display, reinforcing the star's presence as special and extraordinary because of her ability to attract attention. As Charles Ponce de Leon (2002) suggests, this is central to our contemporary understanding of celebrity: "What distinguishes celebrities from the anonymous mass is visibility, a kind of visibility made possible by the media and shaped by journalistic conventions that make celebrities seem at once extraordinary and real: complex, interesting 'human beings' whose unique talents and gifts are accompanied by traits that are commonplace and familiar to ordinary people" (p. 13). These familiar traits are overwhelmingly gendered, as gossip media routinely focus on the romantic relationships and domestic lives of stars. A quick glance at the headlines in the supermarket checkout line promises the inside scoop on the stars' dating lives, marriages, pregnancies, divorces, and family drama, placing feminine concerns of the private sphere, not their talent, at the center of their images. Gossip weeklies obsess over star bodies through feminized discourses in which female stars' (and rarely, but almost never, male stars') faces, bodies, fashion choices, exercise routines, and dietary habits are exhaustingly picked over and analyzed as evidence of their social value (Fairclough, 2008; Holmes, 2005; Holmes and Redmond, 2006; Meyers, 2011). That is, the work of "being themselves," and importantly the right kind of self, is the main focus of these magazines.

Celebrity weeklies maintain their appeal to ordinariness and authenticity through the reliance on gossip and allegedly unauthorized glimpses of the stars' behind-the-scenes lives. In other words, the celebrity gossip media "are structured on an *institutional divorce* from those in the entertainment industry trying to control publicity" (Gamson, 1994, p. 97, emphasis in original). Their resistance to such control (or at least the perception of such resistance) frames gossip media as having more access to the real precisely because of their unauthorized nature. This sense of resistance to control is presented through discourses of gossip or unauthorized access to the behind-the-scenes truths that the celebrity and her handlers strive to keep concealed or at least controlled (ibid.). The autonomous nature of the celebrity weeklies means they often lack the legitimacy to get direct and exclusive access to A-list celebrities and rely instead on paparazzi photographs and anonymously sourced information ("sources close to the star reveal!") that purport to expose the truth about the real person that is hidden by the other workers. On one hand, this allows celebrity weeklies to claim greater access to the truth *because* of their unauthorized access to the stories that the star and her industry handlers attempt to keep hidden. On the other, this lack of access can also be problematic, as their unauthorized access is often challenged as *not* true precisely because of their gossipy reporting and lack of direct access to the stars they cover. This tension again provides a key space for the emergence of reality stars as important figures within these magazines and, in turn, contemporary celebrity culture.

As always private-focused stars, their images fit seamlessly with the gossip media's emphasis on the ordinary and real self. The feminized nature of the reality television genre means the public image of these individuals inextricably ties them to the concerns of domestic life and personal relationships. Reality cast members need the extratextual media attention to help build their intertextual celebrity capital, extending the visibility of this private self beyond the program and into the public realm of celebrity culture, but they also offer gossip media the claim to authenticity that comes from more direct access to their real lives outside of but certainly in conversation with the program from which they emerge. Reality television cast members, as will be seen in subsequent chapters, routinely grant *Us Weekly* interviews and access that A-list stars rarely do. The magazines, in turn, use this "exclusive" access to help celebrify these ordinary individuals who are just being themselves.

Reality Celebrities in *Us Weekly*

Us Weekly is a typical example of this type of celebrity gossip weekly in the United States, reveling in the pursuit of the question of who the star "really" is through paparazzi photos and gossip talk in ways that both celebrate and mock celebrities as markers of social identity. The magazine can leverage its popularity for some level of access to higher-level stars, particularly at red carpet events or in the occasional more promotional-type interviews with A-listers, but overwhelmingly relies on gossip-style unauthorized access to these stars in their unguarded moments. *Us Weekly* simultaneously celebrates extraordinary celebrity lifestyles—the glamour of luxurious homes and vacations, designer clothes, and red carpet events—and insists that those living this life are ultimately just like us, thus using celebrity culture to reinforce the myth of meritocracy that suggests such lifestyles are available to any ordinary person who works hard and deserves them. As will be explored in more detail in chapter 2, *Us Weekly*'s main focus is on the private-side discourses that highlight celebrities as ordinary people and, crucially, uses this ordinariness to justify—or in some cases, challenge—their celebrity status. Furthermore, the magazine's preoccupation with supposedly ordinary feminine concerns of intimate relationships, family, weddings, and fashion pushes its primarily female audience to identify with celebrities as markers of how to properly cultivate the feminine self within contemporary culture. This focus on ordinariness as a path to extraordinary status or as a marker of deserved extraordinary status is evident in the shift to coverage of reality television celebrities within *Us Weekly* in the early twenty-first century.

I am not arguing that *Us Weekly* transformed ordinary individuals into celebrities simply by covering them. Indeed, Turner (2010) notes that just as a claim to or display of talent is not a guarantee of fame, neither is extratextual media attention: "Sometimes no amount of publicity can generate public interest; at other times, the public reveals a mind of its own in its reactions to a specific individual, no matter what the publicity machine does. There is a tension between these two forces—the commercial industry and the public will—and celebrity cannot be constructed or maintained without both playing some part" (p. 55). But *Us* does provide a crucial space of intertextuality in which the ordinary self of the reality television cast member could move into the extraordinary realm of celebrity. However, this process is incomplete and not guaranteed, as not all reality cast members will become celebrities, and many of those that do tend to have a more fleeting relationship with fame tied to the broadcast run of the program from which they emerge. For example, *Us Weekly*'s first major coverage of reality programs and cast members began in 2000 with the first season of *Survivor*, itself one of the first narrative-style reality television programs of this new era to top the prime-time ratings in the United States. This coverage seemed designed to produce celetoids, as it focused primarily on the show itself, tracking narrative developments from week to week and speculating on who would emerge the winner. While the castaways' lives before appearing on *Survivor* were discussed, highlighting their status as ordinary people, most quickly faded into obscurity once their season ended because the magazine did not also offer them space to perform the contrasting celebrity lifestyle labor needed to bring their ordinariness outside of the confines of the program. The season 1 winner, Richard Hatch, did achieve some longevity in terms of continued coverage after the show ended but primarily appeared in *Us Weekly* to discuss the show itself. He was tapped to write a wrap-up/predictions column about season two called "The Hatch Report," in which he, as a former winner, was framed as an expert on the game, thus tying fame to the program in ways that reinforce the low intertextual capital of the celetoid.

However, beginning in the early 2000s, *Us Weekly* pioneered coverage of reality television and developed a stable of reality celebrities who provided reliable ongoing gossip narratives that both tied to and extended beyond their respective reality television programs, notably Trista (Rehn) Sutter and Jenn Schefft from *The Bachelor*/*Bachelorette*, Lauren Conrad and Heidi Montag from *The Hills*, and, late in the decade, the Kardashians. By highlighting the intertextuality of the image—using the reality television program as a space of public performance that is counterbalanced by coverage of the offstage and real self in the magazine—the more enduring form of extraordinarily ordinary star emerged.

From the political economy perspective discussed in the introduction, the rise of the extraordinarily ordinary celebrity helped stabilize the print celebrity gossip media industry during the economic recession and in the face of technological and social changes associated with new media threatening their role in celebrity culture. By expanding the emphasis on the private as a reason for fame, not just a component of it, a whole new range of celebrities could be reliably trotted out to fill *Us Weekly*'s pages with content that reinforced the magazine's commercial and ideological aims. So while many, if not most, of the specific reality celebrities may still be dispensable, the category itself is increasingly central to the operation of twenty-first century celebrity media and culture. Nevertheless, a few individuals emerged as the highest form of extraordinarily ordinary, transcending their reality television roots while maintaining a lasting celebrity tied to just being yourself. Ultimately, this shift toward the private self and the labor of ordinariness as a core tenet of fame has implications for the cultural power of the traditional celebrity, whose claims to talent are increasingly overpowered by media attention to the minutiae of their daily lives. This book aims to explore the distinct parameters of the category of reality celebrity as a figure balancing between the extraordinary and the ordinary and to unpack the sort of ordinary self that is celebrified within the pages of the magazine. I argue that the reality celebrity's presence in *Us Weekly* places her in a complex and liminal space in relation to larger celebrity culture, and one that speaks to the necessary reconceptualization of the tensions between the extraordinary and ordinary selves and the forms of labor that produce celebrity within and across popular media. This form of celebrity helps reaffirm a hierarchy of celebrity that rests on hegemonic norms of race, class, gender, and sexuality by offering a narrow definition of the right kind of self that is worthy of celebrity value.

CHAPTER 2

THE LABOR OF ORDINARINESS

FAMOUS FOR BEING YOURSELF

Ordinariness is a discursive construction that is uniquely deployed in the production and circulation of reality television celebrities, but the attention to the private and ordinary self within extratextual media has long been a central component of celebrity culture. In his landmark study of "biographies" published in popular magazines at the turn of the twentieth century, Leo Lowenthal (1944/2006) identified a key shift in reporting about prominent figures. He claims, "While once it was rather contemptible to give much room to the private affairs and habits of public figures, this topic is now the focus of interest" (p. 133). Magazine profiles were dominated by "idols of consumption," exemplified by the Hollywood star as the "center of this new consumerist heroism" (Gamson, 1994, p. 28). Instead of focusing on the talent or skill that may have brought a star into the public eye, these profiles instead offered reporting on star's "private lives and personal habits, their tastes, romances, likes, and dislikes," highlighting the lavish and glamorous life of leisure afforded by fame (ibid.).

Joshua Gamson (1994) argues that beginning in the 1930s, however, this coverage of the private lives of stars "underwent a gradual demotion of sorts" in which the glamorous lifestyle coverage was subsumed by attention to the ordinary pleasures and values that stars shared with the readers (p. 29). Stars became just like us, embodying the same basic values and desires as the audience—or, more accurately, helping to emphasize what those basic values and desires ought to be—often in contrast to the glamorous facade of fame. These profiles shored up the star's intertextual capital, extending her image across media forms as a means of fortifying her "natural, deserved celebrity" (p. 33). They tell the story of the real off-screen person, providing audiences a space to negotiate the on- and off-screen selves to construct a coherent image. This presents a unique tension for the construction of the reality television celebrity, as her public presence on the reality show, as discussed in the previous chapter, is itself already premised on the revelation of the real and authentic self. The reality cast member needs the extratextual coverage to build the intertextual capital that promotes fame, but it would seem that such coverage lacks the necessary private/public tensions on which celebrity images are traditionally constructed because audiences have already seen the real self on the program.

However, Su Holmes (2004a) argues, the intensification of ordinariness within contemporary celebrity culture enables a deeper negotiation of the real and authentic self across intertextual spaces that has helped to turn the reality television cast member into a celebrity. Holmes highlights the importance of the economic and social relationships between reality television and gossip media in the construction and circulation of ordinary celebrity images, claiming, "While such intertextual relations are not of course new to television, Reality TV has represented an acceleration of their 'synergy'" (p. 121). The show may introduce the reality television cast member into the public eye, but her status as a celebrity is only reached through the continued negotiation of the real individual and the ideological norms of identity she embodies in the extratextual media. Following Holmes, this chapter calls for a reconsideration of the role of intertextuality in the construction of the extraordinarily ordinary celebrity by tracing two key modes of *Us Weekly*'s coverage of reality television cast members: the cyclical celetoid and the grow-your-own celebrity. Through these two modes of coverage, I argue, *Us Weekly*'s negotiation of the private and ordinary self both on and off the show highlights the new centrality of ordinariness to celebrity culture that precipitates the rise of the extraordinarily ordinary celebrity.

The first mode of coverage is the construction of the reality television cast member as a celetoid, emphasizing first the use of the image to promote the program during its broadcast run. Relatedly, I argue, the formulaic nature of reality television programming and that of *Us Weekly*'s gossip narratives open space for a distinct form of this reality celetoid that I call the cyclical celetoid. As with traditional forms of celetoids described by Rojek (2001), the reality cast member's initial presence in *Us Weekly* is as a media-produced celebrity commodity with a short shelf life tied to the broadcast run of the program from which she emerged. The off-screen self on offer in *Us Weekly* does little to extend her persona beyond the narrative boundaries of the show, and she is "easily replaced by the next group [of cast members] if the format is to successfully reproduce itself, series after series" (Turner, 2010, pp. 13–14). The replicability of this type of ordinary celebrity, or the cyclical nature of these celetoids, connects the economic interests of the program and the magazine around the reproduction of particular narratives of the self without a deeper investment toward constructing a lasting celebrity image. In other words, coverage of individual cast members from programs like *The Bachelor/Bachelorette* or *Survivor* is typically framed around the replication of a celebrity type rather than the cultivation of a distinct celebrity image. As this coverage is primarily centered on reinforcing the real person as constructed on the show, the cyclical celetoid also reconceptualizes the public or on-screen side of celebrity image, eschewing the traditional notions of creative labor as the core of the image in favor of an intensification of attention to the labor of ordinariness at all points.

Some individual reality cast members, however, do achieve a longer-lasting and greater level of fame that moves beyond the more simplistic promotional cyclical celetoid mode. This points to the second category of extraordinarily ordinary celebrity in *Us Weekly*: the grow-your-own celebrity whose fame extends beyond the promotional cycle and is predominantly maintained through the magazine's narratives about her private life within its established gossip formulas. Building on both Rojek's (2001) concept of the celetoid and Turner's (2010) argument that the demotic turn's shift toward the celebrification of ordinary individuals reveals the ways in which media "have begun to produce celebrity *on their own*," I argue that the magazine becomes the primary rather than extratextual site of the image (p. 15, emphasis in original). As its coverage shifts away from the more strictly promotional narratives of early reality television coverage, *Us Weekly* grows its own celebrities by moving the cast member outside the textual boundaries of the program and slotting them into the formulaic narratives of real and ordinary selves that shape the magazine's celebrity content. Although the individual does not completely lose her tie to the program from which she originated, the dominant role of defining the image shifts toward the magazine. Rather than being "more or less content to pick up celebrities" produced by the entertainment institutions, *Us Weekly* begins to play a much more active role in the production of a more durable extraordinarily ordinary celebrity that fits neatly within its social and commercial goals (Turner, 2010, p. 15).

Turner specifically cites the rise of reality television programming and its emphasis on ordinariness as an industrial strategy that "enables television producers to 'grow their own' celebrities and to control how they are marketed before, during and after production—all of this while still subordinating the achieved celebrity[1] of each individual to the needs of the particular programme or format" (ibid.). Though Turner describes this increased propensity to "grow your own celebrity" as diversifying the type of celebrities produced—namely, individuals whose images are rooted in ordinariness and authenticity rather than talent and glamour—he asserts that celebrity culture remains a hierarchical system controlled by and for the commercial interests of the media industry. In the case of the reality celebrity, the reality television producers (including the show's producers and the network on which it airs) and *Us Weekly* (as with other extratextual media) have particular, and at times competing, interests in growing the ordinary individual into a celebrity, thus pointing to the hierarchy within extraordinarily ordinary celebrity that mirrors traditional celebrity hierarchies.

Reality Celetoids

Promotional Celetoids

Celebrities play a vital and complex role in the economics of media industries. Dyer (1986) argues that one key element of their economic importance is "market function," in which stars perform in media texts and their images are used to help promote those texts (and a range of related cultural products) (p. 5). In this market function view, the extratextual circulation of reality cast members is ultimately about the promotion of the program through their images, since "increasing an entertainer's notoriety" is a strategy to "increase the likelihood of consumption" of the media text in which the individual performs (Gamson, 1994, p. 63). Such coverage is not strictly about the program; rather, it is about the development of a celebrity persona—that real person who exists behind the performer seen on-screen. Nevertheless, such attention to this real person is a promotional move primarily intended to draw audiences back to the media text. Speaking of film stars, Dyer (1986) asserts, "Stars are part of the way films are sold. The star's presence in a film is a promise of a certain kind of thing that you would see if you went to see the film" (p. 5). Since the reality cast members are ordinary people whose only presence in the media is on the reality program, the development of their personas in *Us Weekly* is, at least initially, about promising audiences what they will see when they watch the program. The magazine coverage provides intertextual capital but does little to construct the image beyond that program, thus constructing these celebrities as promotional celetoids.

The first ever *Us Weekly* cover story devoted to reality television appeared on August 21, 2000, and featured the finalists of the first season of *Survivor*, whose record-breaking ratings made it the surprise hit of the summer television season (Kissell, 2000). This cover story was published the week before the highly anticipated season finale and promised readers insight into the "real lives" of final six contestants, anointing them "the biggest, and unlikeliest, *celebs* of the summer" (Jones & Pappas, 2000, p. 57, emphasis mine). This story was typical of *Us Weekly*'s initial promotional-style coverage of reality television at the start of the decade. First, it featured multiple cast members on the cover, thus increasing the media visibility of the entire cast or set of finalists, not a single individual, as a way to promote the program. Furthermore, it focused on these cast members' labors of ordinariness primarily as a means to enhance and extend the audience's engagement with the program itself rather than build an individual's celebrity persona outside of the narrative goals of the program. The premise of *Survivor* rests on the notion that the successful castaway is not simply succeeding at individual challenges within the program but succeeding at "the overarching game of *Survivor* itself—whose objective is to 'outwit, outplay, outlast' the other players" (Haralovich & Trosset, 1992, p. 72). Thus, the magazine does not necessarily have to reinforce a coherent image of a castaway to remain tied to the narrative but may instead offer counternarratives that nevertheless reinforce the ordinary self seen on the show. Through interviews with "their friends, teachers and colleagues," this first cover story offered deeper insight into how these castaways might be "playing the game," thus drawing audiences back to the program armed with this new insight to the castaways' real selves (Jones & Pappas, 2000, p. 57). The article suggests, for instance, that the castaway Kelly Wiglesworth "comes across as one of the most serious of the remaining *Survivors*" but notes that her older sister Michele Wheatcraft declares her to be "very headstrong and always a little wild" (p. 59). Wiglesworth is described as having developed survival skills growing up in the country but maintaining a vulnerable side that makes other castaways "feel protective of her" (p. 59). While the article falls short of suggesting her on-screen persona is an act solely constructed to play the game, the contrasting views of her real self in the magazine draw audiences back to the show in pursuit of the real Wiglesworth on the show.

It is within these promotional celetoid narratives that reality cast members of color are given the rare opportunity to appear on the cover of *Us Weekly*. Of the sixty-one main cover stories and eighty-five second-level cover stories featuring reality television cast members that appeared between 2000 and 2009, only five main cover stories and four second-level cover stories featured a person of color. Four of those five main cover stories were either the full cast (*Survivor* season 2 cast on January 29, 2001, and *Temptation Island* full cast on February 12, 2001) or finalist covers (*Survivor* season 2 final four on March 12, 2001, and *American Idol* season 2 final three on May 26, 2003) with only one main cover story featuring a solo person of color, *The Biggest Loser* season 6 winner, Michelle Aguilar, who is Latinx, on January 5, 2009. All of these appearances were promotional celetoid narratives, as it was the show—not the individual cast members—that was the primary focus of most of the cover story. This is in line with the broader framing of race in *Us Weekly* through postracial discourses that recognize and celebrate diversity through the inclusion of people of color within its coverage of celebrity culture while obfuscating the centrality of whiteness as the price of admission to this celebrity place. Celebrities of color do appear within the pages of *Us Weekly* but typically only when their bodies and behaviors reinforce white standards of beauty and comportment that already dominate celebrity culture. Even Aguilar's solo appearance coincided with both the premiere of a new season of *The Biggest Loser* and the magazine's annual diet-focused cover story (see the discussion of the publishing schedule in the introduction) and worked to promote the narrative of proper bodily discipline that marks much of the magazine's attention to (white) women's bodies rather than build her individual persona beyond the scope of the reality program.

Us Weekly's role in reinforcing the whiteness of celebrity culture is also evident in the fact that during the time of this study, the magazine never published any level of cover story with stars from reality television programs that featured predominantly black casts, such as VH1's *Flavor of Love* (2006–2008) or *I Love New York* (2007–2008), despite the popularity of these programs.[2] *Flavor of Love*, a dating competition show akin to *Us Weekly* favorite *The Bachelor*, starring rapper Flavor Flav and a contestant pool that was almost exclusively comprised of women of color, was one of the break-out hits of mid-2000s reality television. The season two finale drew "7.52 million total viewers and ranked as the top show of the night and the highest rated non-sports telecast in basic cable for the year in the 18–49 demo" (Becker, 2006). In comparison, the most watched episode of the MTV docusoap *The Hills*, whose cast members appeared on multiple covers around the same period, garnered only 4.8 million viewers (Stetler, 2008). While both programs were considered hits for their respective networks and offered a logical place for *Us Weekly* to pursue at least promotional celetoid-style coverage, that the African American reality television cast members never found traction as cover stories reinforces the ways in which whiteness shapes *Us Weekly*'s coverage of reality television celebrity even at the most basic promotional level. That is, the women of *The Hills* modeled the right kind of ordinary self for *Us Weekly*'s existing narratives, while the women of *Flavor of Love* were too "ghetto" and thus fell outside of the boundaries of celebrity as defined by the magazine.

Supporting the Show's Narrative. The promotional celetoid is the initial result of the successful development of intertextual capital for the reality television cast member. Holmes (2004a), following Barbara Klinger's work on intertextual circulation, maintains that offering "'multiple avenues' of access" to the reality television program is an economic and social strategy to connect it and its cast members as extensively as possible to audiences (p. 121). The intertextual circulation of the reality cast member's image across the show and the magazine matters because it provides the necessary counterbalance of on- and off-screen selves that drives the construction of celebrity. As an extratextual source, the primary role of *Us Weekly* in this relationship is to build the persona through attention to the off-screen self. This narrative is at least initially consistent with the on-screen self, embodying what Dyer (1986) calls "coherent continuousness" that reinforces that "the star really is what she or he appears to be" but works to extend that image in new ways that help intensify it as the authentic or real self (p. 11).

Though she would go on to develop greater celebrity in the pages of *Us Weekly*, the bachelorette Trista Rehn began her celebrity life as a promotional celetoid. The magazine's early coverage of her routinely claimed insider access, offering greater details about the happenings on the show and Trista's weekly elimination of suitors, but did not challenge the program's overall framing of her as a good girl looking for love because this image already fits neatly into *Us Weekly*'s attempt to appeal to female readers through a focus on romantic relationships. A January 27, 2003, article promises "juicy on-set secrets" of the show as told by the producer Lisa Levenson and host Chris Harrison. While their roles as workers on the show give them authority, their insights do little to subvert the narrative goals of the program and the ordinary Trista it offers. For example, Levinson says Trista is "never shy when it comes to kissing or public displays of affection. . . . It's not slutty though. She handles it tactfully and romantically" (Bartolomeo, 2003, January 27, p. 59). A subsequent "*The Bachelorette*'s Diary" piece in the February 24, 2003, in the lead up to the finale has Trista, in her own words (which itself positions *Us Weekly* as an exclusive site for such real insights straight from the star herself), offering unseen details about her trips with the two finalists, including what happened in the "fantasy suite" when cameras were not present. Of her date with (eventual runner-up) Charlie, she says, "You didn't see us on Jet Skis, but it was great (I loved doubling up on the same one!). That night we held hands a lot (his are so strong). What went on behind closed doors that night? After a long day in the sun, I passed out after 15 minutes" (Rehn, 2003, p. 72). In both of these examples, Trista is just being herself, and each space offers a different yet consistent performance of that self.

However, even in the construction of promotional celetoids, the magazine does not simply serve as a mouthpiece for the program's producers. Rather, the magazine must offer something *more* than just a reiteration of what was seen on the program. Indeed, as one of the primary pleasures of both reading gossip and watching reality television is the negotiation of fact and fiction, truth and artifice, "actual" reality and producer intervention, the celebrity image becomes a way the two texts may play off of each other to promote such pleasures. This is not to suggest audiences are dupes, as most know to take both reality television and gossip media's claims of truth with a grain of salt. But Holmes (2004a) claims gossip media here relies on its position as "outsider" to the manufactured on-screen image as a key way to begin to differentiate itself from the show and take over the construction of the real celebrity persona. In her analysis of *Big Brother*, she claims popular press coverage of the housemates separates itself from the program by "claim[ing] to offer a higher form of 'truth' on the programme, the 'reality,' as it were, 'behind' the reality" (Holmes, 2004a, p. 122). This site of tension between the magazine and the program remains a promotional strategy, as the reality cast member's real self in the magazine is always tied back to the show through articles that construct the celebrity image through deeper insight into events already seen or looking ahead to future developments, as with the Trista and *Survivor* examples above. But it enables the magazine to take greater control over (and potentially profit from) the celebrity image by deploying it within its own formulaic narratives in ways that begin to challenge the show's exclusive appeal to the real.

Challenging the Show's Narrative. In this way, *Us Weekly* implicitly, or in some cases explicitly, undermines the claims to truth that underscore the narratives of reality television as a means to construct a celebrity image for a cast member. This is most apparent when *Us Weekly* actively contradicts what happens on the show in ways that claim producers are interfering with the truth (via editing, for example) and that the real story can only be found in the magazine's coverage. For example, an interview with the *Joe Millionaire*[3] finalist Sarah Kozer, published as the season moved toward the finale, directly referenced a scandalous moment from the show when Kozer and Evan Marriott were shown sneaking off into the woods and were heard, but not seen, having what seemed to be a sexual encounter. A sidebar to the main article asks, "How Far Did Their Nooky *Really* Go?" over a series of stills depicting the event with Kozer quoted as saying, "It was an inaccurate portrayal. All I've ever done is kiss Evan," suggesting that unfair editing by the producers was responsible for her hypersexualized image on the show (Baker & Coats, 2003, p. 10). Whereas the program clearly framed Kozer as the gold digger, who reinforced negative stereotypes about women as shallow and manipulative, the three articles that offered in-season coverage of Kozer in *Us Weekly* deftly negotiated that image in ways that engaged the pleasurable salaciousness of her "minxy" image constructed on the show and challenged it as a manipulation on the part of the editors. In other words, it offered readers the opportunity to negotiate the ordinary Kozer constructed on the show with the one on offer in the magazine, thus drawing audiences to both media texts in pursuit of the real image.

A second-level cover story published the week before the season finale promised readers a look "Inside the Tense Finale Catfight: What You Didn't See on TV," a headline that seems to reinforce the good girl / bad girl dichotomy already established on *Joe Millionaire*. However, echoing the traditional intertextual negotiation of the public/private selves that grounds celebrity images, the article itself moves back and forth between framing Kozer as inauthentic and manipulative (e.g., the show's butler/host Paul Hogan is quoted as saying, "Sarah was sincerely genuine . . . in trying to win!") and as an ordinary person who is simply a victim of reality television editing (Pappas, 2003, February 24, p. 49). The article reminds readers of her scandalous on-show image by rehashing the alleged off-screen sexual encounter with Marriott while also explicitly refuting it as a trick of the show's producers. A "pal," Kerry Stenberg, is quoted as saying, "Sarah said [the audio] was taken from a clip where [fellow contestant] Melissa M. was giving her a backrub and she asked if she should lie down" (p. 49). Kozer herself reveals, "One of my coworkers said, 'It's funny that they're portraying you as a gold digger because you are the patron saint of loser guys'" (p. 50). Additionally, it references a scandal previously covered by *Us Weekly* in which it was discovered that Kozer had appeared in foot fetish films during college (Baker & Coats, 2003). But in the magazine's efforts to lay claim to the real Kozer, it reinforces the innocence of this experience by first suggesting it was a "modeling" job to help her financially as she "always lived pay check to pay check," reflecting an economic struggle relatable to many young women (ibid.). The article also fortified the authenticity of Kozer's image by quoting her mother, a presumably reliable source on the real Kozer: "[Kozer had] been starring in fetish films to earn extra cash, which shocked her parents less than *Joe's* subtitled slurp fest. 'The modeling, she owns it,' says Sarah's mother. 'But the way [the producers] made it seem like she had sex in the bushes!'" (ibid.).

This intertextual struggle around the authenticity of Kozer's image thus grounds her celebrity in the labor of ordinariness, as audiences are encouraged to negotiate in which media text she is really just being herself. But it also demonstrates how the magazine seeks to control the celebrity image by claiming access to the real and ordinary self. Despite this battle over the truth, the magazine and the program are still allied in the use of the image to promote the program. That is, it is important to keep in mind that this negotiation is about drawing audiences to the finale, as all the coverage occurred in the weeks leading up to the final episode, and Kozer all but disappeared from the pages of *Us Weekly* after she lost to "good girl" Zora Aldrich.[4]

Promotion between Seasons. Through the intertextual exposure on the show and in the magazine, reality television cast members are constructed into a promotional celetoid level of celebrity, one whose attention capital is manufactured through visibility on the program and in the magazine and whose celebrity typically disappears shortly after the season or program ends. But given the cyclical nature of reality television programming, particularly game-docs, which repopulate program casts each season, *Us Weekly*'s attention to promotional celetoids also became cyclical as a means to cash in on a show's (not a particular celebrity's) popularity. For instance, since season 1 of *Survivor* was one of the most popular television programs of that year, the expansion of *Us Weekly*'s coverage of the next batch of *Survivor* celetoids in season 2 is not particularly surprising. The first season of *Survivor* appeared in *Us Weekly* just three times during its broadcast run, with the most attention occurring with the aforementioned (and only) cover story tied to the finale. Now that the program was established as a hit, the season 2 coverage intensified, with the program and its cast members appearing as the main cover story four times during the course of the season and the weekly developments rehashed in a quarter-page article called "The Hatch Report" (written by season 1 winner, Richard Hatch) four times during the season (March 19, March 6, April 2, and April 9, 2001). The tone of this coverage and the attention to the cast remained deeply tied to the promotion of the program rather than the individual cast members, but the turn to a new crop of castaways points to the start of the cyclical celetoid mode of celebrification.

Season 2's first cover story helped promote the show prior to its premiere through an "exclusive 36-hour October visit to the *Survivor II* set," in which the reporter Ben Pappas dished behind-the-scenes secrets about the conditions of shooting the show, such as a list of provisions and equipment provided to each team and the expanded tribal-council set that "took three months to build and required 28 tons of sand and cement to be hand carted to a remote waterfall" (Pappas, 2001, January 29, p. 46). The article also hinted at upcoming narrative twists, such as the gross-out insect "buffet" challenge, as a way to draw audiences back to the show (p. 46). The coverage of the new cast functioned in a similarly show-focused promotional way, with sidebars introducing each cast member and assessing their chances of winning based on their real selves. The contestant Amber Brkich is described as "no stranger to survival politics: Her grandfather Michael Brkich was the longtime mayor of Bridgewater, Pennsylvania," and Kel Gleason's bio suggests that "his military skills will be a plus on the show, his looks won't hurt either" (p. 51). The magazine does not challenge the program's framing of the contestants here, but it does differentiate itself from that framing through the appeal to the off-screen (and, in this case, prescreen) selves. Readers are thus encouraged to turn back to the program to see how these real people will endure the challenges of the island and perform these identities to, as the show's tagline suggests, "outwit, outplay, outlast" the competition.

It is not until the final cover for this season on May 21, 2001, that any gestures are made to take the cast members out of the program's narrative and into celebrity culture. This is accomplished by combining the cast members' labor of ordinariness with celebrity lifestyle labor, notably in a sidebar titled "Is There Life after *Survivor*?" detailing every cast member's upcoming media appearances and future projects (Milter, 2001, p. 35).[5] Nevertheless, as season 3 approached, *Us Weekly*'s coverage predictably shifted toward the new group of castaways, again using their images to promote the show itself rather than to create a separate celebrity image. As reality television as a genre became more popular with television audiences, it provided *Us Weekly* with a steady stream of personalities that would appeal to readers but without having to invest too much in the expansion of their images. I argue *Us Weekly*'s routine use of these types of reality television celetoids creates a unique form—the cyclical celetoid—that is essential to defining the increasingly important role played by the magazine in the celebrification of the reality cast member.

Cyclical Celetoids

The reality celebrity seems to be the quintessential celetoid, whose media-produced fame is here today and gone tomorrow. Rojek (2001) claims, "Evanescence is the irrevocable condition of celetoid status, though in exceptional cases a celetoid may acquire a degree of longevity" (p. 22). While some fans may fondly remember a favorite contestant or continue to follow her/him on social media after the season ends, most of these celebrities largely drop off the map of mainstream celebrity gossip media like *Us Weekly*. That is, these celebrities may have residual fame or a microcelebrity status that endures with a small fan base, but these sorts of reality stars do not remain visible within mainstream celebrity culture. While individual reality celetoids do often quickly fade away, the synergy between reality television and *Us Weekly* has pioneered the perseverance of a specific *category* of celetoid—for example, the *Bachelor* contestant, the *Big Brother* housemate, *or the Survivor* castaway—that is made and remade in highly routinized and predictable ways in accordance with the narrative of the show from which they emerge *and* that fit within the magazine's narrative focus on private and domestic lives of celebrities.

Gamson (1994) claims that the marketing logic that dominates the circuit of celebrity production ensures that those celebrities who rise to the top are those who can be successfully tailored to (or help construct) audience desires and the needs of commercial enterprises. But this is not an easy process, as celebrity producers can never fully control whether a particular individual will resonate with audiences. Based on his interviews with a range of publicity industry workers, Gamson argues that the successful production of celebrity rests largely on "selecting a marketable aspirant. . . . Confidence in the consumption-readiness of a product [celebrity] . . . saves them and their companies from costly and time-consuming product-improvement activities" (p. 71). The cyclical celetoid as a category helps alleviate some of the struggle in connecting the celebrity image to audiences by inserting new individuals, typically from established reality franchise hits, into *Us Weekly*'s already proven and profitable narrative formulas and ideological frameworks rather than starting from scratch. Thus, *The Bachelor* contestant becomes *The Bachelor* star simply by slotting each new individual into established narratives of heteronormative and hyperfeminine romance and relationships that dominate *Us Weekly*'s coverage of celebrity more broadly and this show specifically. As will be seen with some examples later in this chapter and in chapter 3, the cyclical celetoid may be an end result of media-produced reality television fame, but it can also be a stepping stone for a more lasting grow-your-own-celebrity fame based on the successful performance of the labor of ordinariness in the magazine.

The Bachelor/Bachelorette *Star as Cyclical Celetoid*

The ordinary celebrities emerging from *The Bachelor* and *The Bachelorette* offer a prime example of how the cyclical celetoid is constructed for the mutual benefit of the program and the magazine and how *Us Weekly* grows some of these cyclical celetoids into more lasting and legitimate levels of fame by going beyond the boundaries of the program's narrative. The first season of *The Bachelor* received minimal coverage in the magazine, with only a few mentions of it appearing in the television section during its broadcast run. However, the show's popularity quickly exploded, with season 1 ranking number one in the key eighteen–forty-nine demographic by the end of the season, and coverage subsequently increased in the magazine as well (Collins, 2002). After the finale aired on April 25, 2002, *Us Weekly*'s May 13, 2002, issue included a feature interview with the winner, Amanda Marsh, and the bachelor, Alex Michel, discussing their relationship both on and off the show.[6] The article combined the sort of behind-the-scenes details about the program itself, addressing how the couple fell for each other during the run of the show, with "professional" insight from "relationship experts" about "Amanda's winning ways and how the two runners-up screwed up" (Pappas & Hong, 2002, p. 45). This minimal initial coverage used Marsh's and Michel's images to promote the show, reminding viewers of the romantic relationship that emerged from / was created by the show. Celebrity weeklies have covered the real life romances of achieved stars who met on set, such as the *Twilight* stars Kirsten Stewart and Robert Pattinson or Angelina Jolie and Brad Pitt, but the difference here is these two were on a program *designed* to end in a romantic relationship. Thus, from the beginning, *Us Weekly*'s coverage of *The Bachelor* has functioned as a paratext that extends the audience's engagement with the program's narrative and also helped build celebrity status through the continued coverage of the winning couple's relationship outside that narrative. Though Marsh and Michel's relationship was short-lived and received only scant attention in the magazine, the formula of the show offered a steady stream of ordinary individuals looking for love, which fit directly into the romance narratives that are central to *Us Weekly*. Put differently, the individual *Bachelor/Bachelorette* celetoids could fade away, but the category became an important vehicle for marketing the show and the making and remaking of the normative ideologies about identity—particularly gender—that already dominated *Us Weekly*'s coverage of celebrity culture.

Dyer (1998) argues that what is most crucial about stars is that they "relate to social types of society . . . a shared, recognizable, easily grasped image of how people are in society (with collective approval or disapproval built into it)" (p. 47). Instead of focusing on how an individual relates to this social type, the cyclical celetoid highlights the social type itself as a form of celebrity status by foregrounding the gossip narratives in predictable and easily replicable ways. In short, it is not the individual star that matters but the ability to replicate the heteronormative narrative of romantic love that resonates with the magazine's readers. Beginning with the season 2 bachelor, Aaron Buerge (2002), and the season 1 bachelorette, Trista Rehn (2003), *Us Weekly* was the primary extratextual source for "official" insider access to every season of *The Bachelor* or *The Bachelorette. Us Weekly*'s subsequent coverage of the various *Bachelor/Bachelorette* seasons proceeds in nearly identical fashion: preseason coverage, in-season narratives, postfinale interview, and postseason relationship coverage, all of which allows readers to follow the narrative of an ordinary individual who is inserted into feminized fantasies of romance and marriage. This emphasis on ordinariness was typically displayed through a personal interview or via "inside scoop" from friends and family that highlights the cast member as an ordinary person looking for love. These insider looks tend to, at least during the show's broadcast run, reinforce the continuity of the image across the show and the magazine.

Though heralded as the driving force behind *Us Weekly*'s zeitgeist-defining content, Janice Min, in an interview from 2018, maintained that the decision to cover *The Bachelor* actually originated with the publisher Jann Wenner. She claimed Wenner was "obsessed with" *The Bachelor* and suggested she put the season 3 bachelor, Andrew Firestone, on the cover on a "crazy whim" because Wenner "believed in him" (WNYC Studios, 2018).[7] That "whim," of course, helped the magazine once again drive the cultural narrative, as that cover (June 2, 2003), Min declared, was "the highest selling issue of *Us Weekly* at that time" and helped establish the franchise as central to the magazine's gossip formulas (ibid.). Whether it was Min or Wenner who made the initial call, *Us Weekly*'s increasing coverage of *The Bachelor* franchise across the decade both benefitted from and contributed to the program's growing popularity with television audiences. According to Rachel E. Dubrofsky (2006), *The Bachelor* was broadly popular, with the first five seasons averaging 11.3–16.7 million viewers. Thus, it makes sense that a magazine focused on celebrity culture would look to this increasingly popular media franchise as a source for content. However, under the logics of contemporary media conglomeration, the attention to the cast members from *The Bachelor* and *The Bachelorette* was likely also the result of Disney's corporate ownership, as the franchise aired on Disney-owned ABC. Though I can find no evidence of exclusive contracts binding these cast members to do interviews only with *Us Weekly*, the magazine's first, if not exclusive, access to each season's cast members suggests a close relationship between corporate siblings ABC and *Us Weekly* in helping to grow the popularity of the franchise and its cast members. While some of these individual cast members, notably *The Bachelor*'s Firestone and his fiancée, Jenn Schefft, and *The Bachelorette*'s Trista Rehn (Sutter), did develop more lasting celebrity personas through the continued performance of the labor of ordinariness and the additional performance of celebrity lifestyle labor, as will be discussed, all *Bachelor/Bachelorette* stars initially enter celebrity culture as cyclical celetoids through this formulaic coverage that came to define *Us Weekly*'s attention to the franchise.

In the preseason coverage, readers are invited to "meet the new *Bachelor*" prior to the start of the show's run on ABC and are often also given a glimpse of the cast of women who will vie for the final rose. Of the twelve seasons of *The Bachelor* that aired during the time frame of this study (seasons 2–13), every single new bachelor was introduced in the magazine prior to the start of the show with at least a half-page section, and eight of the seasons introduced him in at least a one-page story. It is typical that these introductions are in the same issue and often for the shorter ones embedded in the same article, as the concluding season's bachelor's or bachelorette's postfinale interview. Like a chain smoker lighting the next cigarette from her last, the end of one cyclical celetoid cycle launches the narrative arc of the next. These introductions are incredibly formulaic, with seven of the twelve introductions headlined either "Meet The New *Bachelor*" or "The New *Bachelor*," and all featured the new *Bachelor* star revealing the kind of woman he is looking for and forwarding the heteronormative and hyperfeminized romance narrative (e.g., finding "the One") that structures both the show and *Us Weekly*'s typical coverage of celebrity couples. In particular, these introductions highlight the bachelor's emotional side over a hypermasculine and macho persona. For instance, the season 6 bachelor, Byron Velnick, says, "Wisdom and intelligence turn me on" and that he is looking for a mature woman because "a 22-year-old girl doesn't know what love is yet" (Mehalic, 2004, p. 62). The season 9 bachelor, Lorenzo Borghese, describes his ideal woman as "someone who is outgoing, funny and understands me" (Agresti, 2006, p. 80). The season 3 bachelor, Firestone, received two preseason introductions in *Us Weekly*. The first appeared in the March 17, 2003, issue in the On the Record section, a regular *Us Weekly* feature of short items announcing celebrity marriages, births, divorces, and, in some cases, upcoming projects. Firestone's blurb included a photo but offered only that he is the twenty-seven-year-old "member of the famous [Firestone] tire family," who works in "sales and marketing for his family's winery, Firestone Vineyard in Santa Barbara, California" (Gallo, 2003, p. 46). Though this initial short introduction was a stand-alone article rather than a sidebar to a story about the current season's star or couple, it is notable that it appeared in an issue that advertised an "exclusive interview" with *Bachelorette* season 1 couple Trista Rehn and Ryan Sutter about their wedding plans on the cover and thus still capitalized on the cyclical celetoid from the franchise to help launch the next.

Firestone's main introduction came two weeks later (the week his season premiered on ABC) in a two-page spread titled "Bring on *The Bachelor* 3" chock full of personal details about the "youngest son of the *shockingly wealthy* Firestone dynasty (think tires and wine)," who is "out to snag a spouse" (Pappas, 2003, March 31, p. 46, emphasis mine). While his wealth is frequently referenced as part of his appeal as a romantic partner, the article primarily frames him as an ordinary and down-to-earth guy looking for the right woman. In particular, as with the other *Bachelor* stars, he highlights his "wish list" for a partner as "a woman with 'a sense of adventure, confidence and a willingness to take a chance'" and promises that "romance comes in strange packages—and it certainly showed up during filming" (p. 46).[8] While these introductory narratives undoubtedly aim to draw readers to watch the show, they also provide the bedrock on which the in-season narrative and postseason narrative coverage of the bachelor's search for love and his post-show relationship that will play out in the magazine. Thus, from the beginning, the *Bachelor* star is a cyclical celetoid constructed around an idealized feminine fantasy of romantic partners, suggesting what the right kind of partner would be for the female readers. This framing is crucial for the male star, as the *Bachelor* star itself is an anomaly within a magazine that primarily focuses on female celebrities and to attract young female readers. In her study of contemporary celebrity weeklies, Andrea McDonnell (2014) confirms that these magazines are "fundamentally concerned with the experiences and emotions of women" and that male celebrities are "featured less often and less prominently than their female counterparts" (p. 7). Male celebrities, she claims, "are rarely the centerpiece of a story," and when a male celebrity is featured, his "import is determined by his relationship to the women in his life" (pp. 7–8). The *Bachelor* star works as a cyclical celetoid because his narrative centers on finding a heterosexual romantic partner, and subsequent coverage centers on the couple more so than the bachelor himself.

After introducing the new bachelor, the week-to-week coverage of the show was limited to the "what you didn't see on TV" mode, typically with the bachelor (or, occasionally, recently ousted contestants) offering the inside scoop on what really happened. Firestone (2003) penned one "*Bachelor*'s Diary," which appeared in the issue published the week season 3 premiered, in which he "reveals his stress" about the first night on the show (where he had to eliminate ten women) and how he found comfort in a toy bus given to him by his nephew (p. 84). Similarly, a mid-season 4 article titled "What the Women Don't Know about Bob" offered deeper personal details about that season's bachelor, Bob Guiney, including that "he loves beauty stuff," that he prefers Dove soap because "as a kid, his naughty deeds . . . were punished with a mouthful of Ivory!" and that he "has a soft side too," evidenced by his love of *It's a Wonderful Life* and admission that he cries every time he watches it (Pappas, 2003, November 3, pp. 56–57). These off-screen details deepen Guiney's image as an ordinary "nice guy" who fits into a heteronormative ideal of a male partner for the female readers. Though they focus on the male stars, these articles simultaneously reinforce the normative femininity forwarded on *The Bachelor* and strengthened in the magazine, particularly around what sort of woman will be successful in achieving a romantic relationship with this ideal man. For instance, the sidebar "*Bachelor*'s Diary" article in the same issue titled "So, Are These Women Crazy?" emphasizes the nice guy narrative while also subtly judging the female contestants' adherence to normative femininity as Guiney compassionately reveals his take on the "extreme behavior" exhibited by some of the women on recent episodes of the show. On cast member Misty's sobbing after her elimination, he says, "It surprised me that Misty was so sad—it broke my heart when I saw her crying. But even though there was a physical attraction, we had never gotten to know each other beyond the surface. I didn't have a chance to explain" (p. 57). These "diaries" are not weekly; nor are they included in the magazine for every season. Even if in-season coverage of a given season is scant, *Us Weekly* reliably returned to coverage of the show as each season neared its final episode. These articles incorporated both promotion narratives and began to signal the potential move of the cast member's image outside of the narrative boundaries of the show through a focus on his or her ordinary off-screen self. In other words, these finale interviews often served to groom the star and/or couple to be grown into lasting celebrities through continued coverage in *Us Weekly*.

Though the magazine always includes some sort of feature on the finalists and the "choice" facing the bachelor in the lead up to the finale, the most important moment of transition for the *Bachelor* stars is the postfinale "exclusive" interview with the new couple (or, in the case of Jen Schefft from season 3 of *The Bachelorette* and Brad Womack from season 11 of *The Bachelor*, where no proposal occurred, with the cast members themselves). During the height of the show's popularity in the early part of the decade, these features were often main cover stories (Firestone and Schefft on June 2, 2003, *The Bachelorette*'s Meredith Phillips and Ian McKee on March 15, 2004, and *The Bachelor*'s Jesse Palmer and Jessica Bowlin on June 7, 2004), but as the popularity of the show dipped somewhat (and, notably, after Disney sold its shares of *Us Weekly* back to Wenner in August 2006), these post-show interviews were reduced to second-level cover stories (such as the *Bachelor* season 6 couple, Byron Velnick and Mary Delgado, on December 13, 2004) or simply one-page Love Lives or other features (such as for the season 7 bachelor, Charlie O'Connell, and Sarah Brice; the season 9 bachelor, Lorenzo Borghese, and Jennifer Wilson; and the season 12 bachelor, Matt Grant, and Shayne Lamas). These articles close the narrative arc of the season, typically demonstrating how the happy couple has found love (the intended goal of the program) and detailing their plans for the future as a couple. Importantly, as previously discussed, the postfinale interview typically begins to shift to the next season's *Bachelor* star by including a sidebar introduction of the next bachelor or bachelorette, thus reminding readers that the show and its romantic narrative will begin again with a new celetoid at the center. The *Bachelor/Bachelorette* cast members continued to be fodder for the magazine throughout the 2010s, with each season's stars appearing at least once as a cover story, as well as in the typical pre/in-/postseason coverage established during the 2000s, reinforcing their viability as cyclical celetoids for the magazine.[9]

This cyclical celetoid level of fame is an important space of initial celebrity visibility in *Us Weekly* and one that, particularly in the case of the *Bachelor* franchise, is all but shut off to reality cast members of color. During the scope of my project, which encompassed the first thirteen seasons of *The Bachelor* and the first five of *The Bachelorette*, not a single person of color was named as the titular bachelor/bachelorette. It was not until season 18 (2014) that *The Bachelor* cast Venezuelan American Juan Pablo Galvais as its first—and, as of this writing, only—bachelor of color and season 12 (2016) for *The Bachelorette* to cast a woman of color in the title role (Iranian American JoJo Fletcher, followed the next season by African American Rachel Lindsay). The franchise has a long history of diversity issues in its casting of contestants as well, as those on both franchises have been and continue to be overwhelmingly white with typically no more than one or two contestants of color included in a particular season and some seasons featuring only white contestants (Fitzpatrick, 2016). For the few people of color who have been cast on these programs, they do not last long. A *Splinter* analysis of the eliminations since the show's debut in 2002 through season 20 in 2016 found that the contestants of color are overwhelmingly eliminated early, with "more than half—59%—of black *Bachelor* and *Bachelorette* contestants" eliminated within the first two weeks of the show (Fitzpatrick, 2016). Given that cyclical celetoid status begins from and relies heavily on participation in the continuing narrative of the program, this lack of diversity in the *Bachelor* franchise's cast directly affects the celebrities who potentially emerge from it.

Moreover, the franchise, and by extension *Us Weekly*'s coverage of it, is governed by a familiar postracial discourse of multiculturalism that, according to Dubrofsky (2006), suggests the show is a neutral space where racial differences "do not exist" as "everyone, ostensibly, can compete to win the rewards of the show—finding a romantic partner" (p. 44). However, such claims that "color does not matter" simultaneously obscure the ways in which this narrative recenters whiteness through the suggestion "that white women and women of color have access to the same choices, will benefit from the same rewards, and suffer the same consequences for the choices they make" (p. 44). That women of color do not typically progress to the end of the season is framed on the show as the result of personal choices and failings rather than tied to larger systemic and cultural contexts that reify whiteness. These same postracial logics extend to *Us Weekly*'s coverage of the show and construction of celebrity from its participants. It is not simply that the women who emerge from these programs as celebrities just *happen* to be white. Rather, the narratives of celebrity that frame *Us Weekly*'s coverage of reality television celebrity, particularly the *Bachelor* franchise, are deeply rooted in a white, heterosexual femininity that suggests it is open to everyone, while only rewarding those whose performance of the ordinary self reinforces the normative center.

For instance, Dubrofsky (2006) discusses the ways in which the *Bachelor* contestant Mary Delgado was effectively "whitened" between her initial appearance on season 4 of the show and her reappearance and eventual win on season 6. She says, "[Cuban American] Mary had appeared in season four, when the series marked her explicitly as Cuban American. In season six her ethnicity was not mentioned until the second-to-last episode. . . . Because she was not marked physically as a woman of color, the series could represent her ethnicity in a mutable fashion" (p. 42). The "mutability" of her ethnicity carried over into the

Us Weekly coverage of her relationship with the season 6 bachelor, Byron Velnick. The couple appeared in a second-level cover story on December 13, 2004, that did the typical postfinale interview work of detailing the couple's romantic "journey" on the show, their deepening relationship after the show ended, and their plans for their future as a couple. Delgado's ethnicity is mentioned twice in the article, once in recounting how Velnick proposed in Spanish on the finale of *The Bachelor* "to make sure [her] parents [Juan and Juanita, who hail from Cuba and do not speak English] could understand" and, second, in highlighting the couple's shared love of cooking in which "she makes Cuban dishes, he whips up fish tacos and guacamole" (Bartolomeo & Dirmann, 2004, p. 69). But the subsequent coverage of the couple, which was confined to just three sidebar mentions and no additional cover appearances,[10] slots the couple into the same postseason narratives that define *Us Weekly*'s coverage of the show without further engaging Delgado's ethnicity. Thus, just as Dubrofsky claims Delgado had her ethnicity erased to fit the narrative of the franchise, so too does *Us Weekly* selectively engage mentions of her ethnicity to highlight diversity but then recuperate such difference back into its normative narratives around whiteness.

Grow-Your-Own Celebrity

Whereas the promotional cyclical celetoid mode ties the on- and off-screen selves almost exclusively to the program, it was with some *Bachelor/Bachelorette* cast members that the persona also began to move outside of the narrative boundaries of the program and more squarely into the narrative formulas of the magazine. In the market logic of the cyclical celetoid, last season's *Bachelor/Bachelorette* star should fade away to make room for the current season's model. Yet *Us Weekly* heavily invested in the continued coverage of several of these cast members and worked to grow their celebrity within the magazine's established gossip formulas. No longer beholden to the show-focused coverage that grounded the cyclical celetoid during the broadcast run of her season, *Us Weekly* began to take over as the dominant space where her image was produced and circulated.

This expansion of the celebrity-building capacity of the magazine speaks to a second and more complex mode of intertextuality discussed by Holmes (2004a). Here the extratextual media moves from promoting the show to constructing a persona independent of that show that nevertheless remains viable for the narratives of ordinariness that structure gossip media. She uses the coverage of *Big Brother* housemates as an example, pointing to the ways in which the British popular media "'raid' the contestants' *past* selves prior to their entrance into the house" in a way that "explicitly rejects the attempt to keep pace with the 'liveness' of the series" and instead constructs their own version of the celebrity image (p. 125). Because the premise of *Big Brother* means that the houseguests are inaccessible to the media during the run of the show, Holmes suggests the gossip magazines construct the off-screen self through interviews with family and friends that purport to offer the real person we may or may not be seeing on the program. This certainly helps promote the program, but it is not explicitly *about* the program and begins to construct the housemates as celebrities whose lives are worth paying attention to by virtue of their performance of the labor of ordinariness outside of, and in this case *before*, the narrative of the program. This bid to control the production and circulation of the celebrity image through coverage of the ordinary self beyond the scope of the show is consistent with Turner's (2010) claim about the media industries' increased propensity to "grow their own" celebrities in ways that support their own economic, social, and cultural goals.

In Holmes's example, this intertextuality is still intended, in part, to lead the audience back to the text to validate the realness of the ordinary self, but it is also a clear bid by the gossip press to lay claim to the authentic celebrity separate from the image seen on the program in ways that support the economic and social goals of the magazines and newspapers themselves. I want to expand Holmes's argument here to recognize *Us Weekly*'s bid to grow its own celebrity through its construction of extraordinarily ordinary celebrity outside the narrative boundaries of the show particularly *after* the show has aired and the cyclical celetoid fame should end. The continued mining of the ordinary individual within the magazine's own formulaic narratives becomes a way *Us Weekly* helps transform a mere celetoid into a more lasting celebrity, one that can reliably fill pages and reinforce the hegemonic cultural norms of identity—namely, whiteness, hyperfemininity, and heteronormativity—that shape its narratives.

Using the raw materials, so to speak, of the *Bachelor/Bachelorette* reality celetoid, the magazine first grew its own celebrity through continued coverage of these ordinary individuals living out the everyday experience of a romantic relationship. This is a more self-conscious bid to promote the magazine's role in creating cultural constructions of identity rather than relying on the program to deliver individuals who embody those ideals. *Us Weekly* even cheekily mocks its own narrative formula in the postfinale interview with Jen Schefft after she refused the proposal of the *Bachelorette* finalist Jerry Ferris: "After eight seasons of *The Bachelor* and *The Bachelorette*, fans have come to expect a few things of the ABC series: The show usually ends with a proposal; the couple reunite postfinale to prove their love; then, in a matter of weeks, they often break up" (Bartolomeo, 2005, p. 107). While this coverage is rooted in the cyclical arc of these particular stars, it moves beyond it through attention to the continued performance of the labor of ordinariness or just being themselves as they embark on a new life together separate from the initial site of public performance of *The Bachelor/Bachelorette*. Though the show may be referenced as the origins of the couple, the magazine is no longer the extratextual source for the construction of celebrity—it has become the text. For the most part, the winning couple's lives are documented *only* in the magazine (and in other celebrity weeklies, but, particularly with the *Bachelor* franchise, *Us Weekly* claims "exclusive" access and personal interviews that are not available in other sources, likely because of Disney's shared ownership). This is not to suggest the magazine created these stars out of nothing, but I argue that *Us Weekly* takes personas that should fade away and, by continuing to insert them into its own feminized formulas of romance and consumerism, extends and, indeed, increases the celebrity of the individual. Put differently, the attention-getting capital that originated on the show is grown through coverage in the magazine, and those cast members whose narratives find a foothold with *Us Weekly*'s female readership begin to move beyond basic celetoid status and into a more lasting celebrity rooted in the continued labor of ordinariness.

As with other celebrities covered by the magazine, readers are encouraged to look to the *Bachelor* star as leading an ordinary life to which one should aspire (or, in some cases, look at as a cautionary tale). But a heightened reality marked by the specialness of celebrity—bestowed by virtue of being in the magazine in the first place—makes their identities even more desirable. Completing the promotional coverage of season 3, *Bachelor* couple Andrew Firestone and Jen Schefft appeared on the cover of *Us Weekly* the week following the season finale of the show. The "exclusive" coverage of "our love story" worked, as most of the postfinale interviews for *The Bachelor* and *Bachelorette* do, to establish the couple as happily in love, reaffirming the romantic narrative forwarded by the show but beginning to take it outside the narrative arc of the show (Pappas, 2003, June 2, p. 44). While Firestone is described as kissing and being physically close to Schefft during photo shoots, the article prioritizes the couple's emotional connection as evidence that they, in the words of the host, Chris Harrison, are "the first [*Bachelor* couple] that got it right" (qtd. in ibid.). Firestone describes Jen as "[having] it all: patience, sense of humor, energy, drive and charisma . . . 'I am so high energy—she is a calming influence,'" and Schefft "marvels at their immediate connection" and sees Firestone as "the One: smart, charming, funny—with the potential to be a great father" (p. 46). Despite having met on a reality program explicitly designed to produce such a coupling, this fact is subordinated to the narrative of an authentically ordinary couple in love, living out the idealized romantic narrative of finding "the One" and planning a life together.

While the postfinale interview signals the end of the more strictly promotional cycle of their celetoid status, Firestone and Schefft continued to appear in the magazine throughout that summer and fall, including one main cover story (June 23, 2003) and three second-level cover stories (June 16, June 30, July 7–14) and multiple appearances in Love Lives and other regular features discussing their ongoing engagement and relationship, culminating in the December 22, 2003, cover story detailing their "surprising" split. The two did appear to reunite, to much celebration by *Us Weekly*, in yet another cover story on February 23,

Figure 3. Firestone/Schefft cover, June 2, 2003.

2004, detailing a dinner date the two shared in Chicago, where Schefft was living after moving out of the couple's San Francisco apartment (Bartolomeo, 2004, February 23). Their breakup was first reported as permanent through a May 3, 2004, cover story that placed Schefft at the center of a love triangle with Firestone and the *Apprentice* winner Bill Rancic after Schefft began dating Rancic (Bartolomeo, 2004, May 3). Their breakup was absolutely final when it was announced, naturally via an *Us Weekly* cover story on December 27, 2004, that Schefft would star on season 3 of *The Bachelorette*. Schefft's enduring celebrity in *Us Weekly* after her initial appearance on *The Bachelor* is here cashed in for a return to reality television in the same franchise that birthed her celebrity status (Bartolomeo, 2004, December 27). This further benefited *Us Weekly* because Schefft, an established celebrity in the magazine, could now be inserted into a new narrative arc as a woman, like many of the magazine's readers, still "looking for love."

Though some efforts at celebrity lifestyle labor are present in these articles, such as the discussion of Schefft's three-carat diamond ring (Pappas, 2003, June 2) and a timeline of media appearances and interviews following the season finale (Youngman, 2003), the main goal of these feature articles is to reinforce the ordinariness of these two stars. For example, the photos that accompany most of the cover stories (including June 2, June 9, and July 7–14, 2003, and February 23 and May 3, 2004; see figure 3 for an example) all show the couple in simple clothing—jeans and T-shirts—that differentiate them from a more glamorous celebrity and remind readers that they are just like us. The stories focused on their relationship detail the "typical" milestones a couple reaches, such as meeting each other's families (June 2, 2003) and moving in together (June 9, 2003). But they also reveled in quotidian relationship details, such as how Schefft and Firestone were learning about each other's quirks, in an article from June 9, 2003:

> Surprise #3: Andrew burped in Jen's ear
> "There's nothing about Andrew that has surprised me yet," says Jen. "I discovered Andrew's quirks early on." Yeah, like his "flirty" burping on their one-on-one date in Scottsdale, Arizona. "Nothing has changed."
>
> Surprise #4: Andrew found out Jen is a klutz
> The signs were all there—Jen has broken her foot twice, and she clumsily dropped her final rose after he got down on one knee. Now Andrew sees the trend. "It's hilarious," he says, laughing. "This morning I was on the phone and she tripped over the cord and almost did a face plant." (Youngman, 2003, p. 50, emphasis in original)

It is this ordinariness and its tie to the gossip formulas that structure the magazine that enable *Us Weekly* to continue to grow Schefft and Firestone as celebrities. What little claim to creative labor or public performance they had on the reality program is now gone, as they were not appearing on any reality television program during the duration of this coverage, and the cyclical arc of *Us Weekly*'s *Bachelor* coverage had already moved on to the season 4 bachelor, Bob Guiney, and his search for love.

As with the cyclical celetoid, growing its own celebrity gives *Us Weekly* a more reliable stream of content and, importantly, a claim to exclusivity and insider access that helps maintain its popularity with readers and place within celebrity culture. The cover stories and interviews position *Us Weekly* as a trusted insider, promising readers the information they will not find in rival publications or upstart gossip blogs. This is not to suggest there was no coverage of this couple and their romantic relationship in other celebrity weeklies at the time, but *Us Weekly* maintained an exclusive relationship with them for interviews that benefitted both the magazine and the stars themselves. In this way, *Us Weekly* simultaneously provided both the on- and off-screen self, rooting both in the performance of the labor of ordinariness. Even after their romantic relationship and thus the peak of their fame ended, the two continued to appear in the magazine alongside other traditional celebrities, most notably in feature articles about their weddings to other noncelebrity people (Firestone in a five-page second-level cover story in the July 21, 2008, issue and Schefft in a six-page second-level cover story in the June 1, 2009, issue) that occurred well after either last appeared on reality television. While this is tied, in part, to the celebrity lifestyle labor that will be discussed in the next chapter, their public performance of themselves as part of a romantic narrative ensured that their images could continue to be utilized in the magazine's gossip narratives.

Trista (Rehn) Sutter as a Grow-Your-Own Celebrity

While the cyclical celetoid mode is premised on the sheer replicability of the category and promises at least a low level of media-produced fame for reality cast members in popular franchises, the grow-your-own mode of celebrity is more elusive because it bestows a higher level of fame. In some ways, it is impossible to predict which reality cast member will capture the audience's attention and be able to transition from celetoid-level fame to the extraordinarily ordinary. It would seem that the individual's ability to fit into the formulaic narratives of *Us Weekly* would be a prime predictor of their ability to achieve greater celebrity, and, as will be seen in the examples below, this is a crucial part of which reality cast members move into celebrity status. However, Dyer's (1998) claim that "there are many cases of stars who are given the full promotion treatment, but do not make it" certainly applies to reality television cast members, including the vast majority of the cast members of *The Bachelor* and *Bachelorette* series whose coverage during and even after the show was not enough to maintain celebrity status even though their romance-based narratives (either as a "successful" couple or tracking them through the heartache of breakup) are relatable to the young female readership of the magazine (p. 14). While Schefft and Firestone succeeded, both as a couple and individually, as grow-your-own celebrities in *Us Weekly*, I argue, the first celebrity to be grown primarily through coverage in *Us Weekly* was the season 1 bachelorette, Trista (Rehn) Sutter, and her image provides an instructive example of the relationship between reality program, magazine coverage, and the move toward lasting extraordinarily ordinary fame based on performing the right kind of ordinary self.

As discussed above, the initial coverage of Trista was closely centered on the narrative developments of *The Bachelorette* in ways that helped promote the show through an appeal to her as an ordinary girl looking for love. An interview with Trista on January 13, 2003, helped promote the start of the *Bachelorette* spin-off (which began on January 8) and began to position Trista as the embodiment of idealized femininity and heteronormativity, as consistent with the program's narrative goals and *Us Weekly*'s celebrity romance narratives. Though she appeared in a celebrity magazine, her love life was always framed in *Us Weekly* as ordinary, positioning her as someone with whom female readers could relate. This performance of the labor of ordinariness or just being herself on the show extended to all coverage of her in *Us Weekly* as well. In an article published the week after the premiere of *The Bachelorette*, Trista is described as the woman "whom [Alex] Michel jilted in the final episode of the *Bachelor*'s first season," framing the new program as Trista's second chance to find true love (Bartolomeo, 2003, January 27). In other words, she is publicly living out the quest all women are presumed to be on—namely, to find a husband. This appeal to her ordinariness as a means to promote the show continued through its broadcast run. Her "*Bachelorette*'s Diary," for instance, appeared as a sidebar article in the February 24, 2003, issue as a space for Trista to offer deeper insight on her one-on-one dates with the two finalists in the week leading up to the show's finale. Here, Trista gives audiences a few details on "what you didn't see" on her final one-on-one dates with the finalists Ryan and Charlie, intimating that she "knows [she] made the right choice, but it was hard" (Rehn, 2003, p. 72). Her diary effectively teases the upcoming finale, but also, in its first-person language, reads like details dished by a girlfriend about her love life.

Tellingly, however, coverage of Trista experienced an uptick *after* the finale had aired, as the magazine continued its coverage of her ongoing romance with fiancé and then husband Ryan Sutter. (Sutter proposed on *The Bachelorette*'s final episode after Trista selected him as the winner.) After her season ended in February 2003 and in the lead up to their wedding in December 2003 (which aired on ABC on December 10, 2003, and is discussed in detail in chapter 3), Trista appeared (with Ryan) as the main cover story two times (September 8 and December 15) and as a second-level cover story six times in 2003 (March 17, March 24, April 7, June 2, June 16, and June 23). The ordinariness helped insert her into the cyclical celetoid narratives in *Us Weekly*, but the continued performance of the "right" kind of ordinariness became the basis for her continued celebrity outside the narrative boundaries of the program. Her grow-your-own celebrity undeniably still worked on a promotional level, as ABC televised the couple's wedding, and thus keeping her in the public eye was a necessary means of marketing this program. Moreover, Trista's narrative of romantic success through the show was harnessed to help promote subsequent seasons, as the ongoing attention to the details of her private life in the magazine reminds viewers of the possibilities promised by *The Bachelor* and *The Bachelorette*.

But the image of Trista forged on *The Bachelorette*, steeped in dominant ideologies of femininity, heteronormativity, and whiteness, began to uncouple from the show and stand on its own with this ordinary self as the core of her fame. That is, she began to appear in the magazine not in specific relation to the show but for just being herself. She became an *Us Weekly* grown celebrity. The magazine continued to track Trista and Ryan's relationship, including items on their Christmas plans in the December 24, 2004, issue and her "Birthday Surprise for Ryan" on October 3, 2005, as well as coverage of her celebrity lifestyle labor, such as her turn on the first season of *Dancing with the Stars* in 2005, another ABC network reality program.[11] Ultimately, she re-emerged as a cover story four years later in 2007, first with the exclusive "first pics" of her and her husband, Ryan, with their new baby boy, Max, and then again in the November 24, 2007, issue with her "diet vow" to lose the baby weight and an "exclusive" follow-up on January 28, 2008, celebrating "How I Got My Body Back." Trista had no public performance on a reality program at this time; thus the magazine had become the primary text through which her image was constructed and circulated. Furthermore, this continued coverage of Trista was steeped in ordinariness, as it did not insinuate that her America's-sweetheart appeal demonstrated on *The Bachelorette* would provide an entry point into the creative labor that traditionally buoys stardom. Instead, the magazine continued to cover Trista just being herself, and helped to solidify a celebrity status based on the performance of the right kind of hyperfeminine and heteronormative self. In short, Trista fit right into the magazine's established formulas for covering female celebrities: beauty, babies, and body. She was ordinary, but the magazine's attention to her ordinariness made her special and worthy of celebrity status. However, as will be seen in the next chapter, the labor of ordinariness alone is not a sufficient means to produce and, importantly, maintain fame in *Us Weekly*. The magazine also highlights the centrality of celebrity lifestyle labor as an important counterbalance to the image that helps move the ordinary celebrity into the level of a more durable extraordinarily ordinary celebrity.

CHAPTER 3

CELEBRITY LIFESTYLE LABOR

MAKING THE ORDINARY EXTRAORDINARY

As reality television became a dominant staple on broadcast and cable television in the early 2000s, it reshaped celebrity culture by offering media visibility to its ordinary cast members. Such visibility, Nick Couldry (2003) argues, is a major space of differentiation between "media people" or those who are visible through the media and the "ordinary people" who are not, a hierarchical distinction that implies simply being visible in the media offers an initial, though not complete, path to celebrity status (p. 108). For reality cast members, ordinariness grounds the public image, both "confirming the 'reality' of what is shown" on the program, thus authenticating the "real" self on offer, and "the status from which the contestants compete to escape into another ritually distinct category, celebrity" (p. 107). Ordinariness may help a cast member become a "media person" through appearance on the reality program as "herself," but in order to transition to the distinct category of "celebrity," the reality cast member must "escape" or become something *more* than *just* ordinary. This presents a certain paradox for the reality cast member—she needs to move away from the ordinary self documented in the program while simultaneously maintaining a connection it. Or, more accurately, to be a celebrity instead of simply a media person, she must find the means to make her ordinary self extraordinary. Lacking the tie to creative labor that lends extraordinariness to the traditional star by highlighting the talent that the real person possesses, the reality cast member must instead find ways to engage her media-person persona in extraordinary ways. It is here that the extratextual media, particularly the celebrity weeklies like *Us Weekly*, are crucial vehicles for the movement of the reality cast member from media person to celebrity.

Extratextual media are already woven into the fabric of celebrity culture. Their coverage of the private self helps expand and circulate the celebrity image in order to build the attention capital that is "cashed in" for future entertainment industry jobs (Gamson, 1994, p. 63). Celebrities and extratextual media exist in a symbiotic yet contentious relationship. Celebrities need visibility, and celebrity weeklies need a steady stream of photos and interviews with stars, the more exclusive the better, to sell issues. Celebrity weeklies like *Us Weekly* help traditional stars increase their value not as platforms for displaying talent but as outlets for the private self, working to humanize the otherwise extraordinary star through glimpses of the real and ordinary self. In this pursuit of the real self, *Us Weekly* often pushes against the tightly controlled star image, using gossip and unauthorized paparazzi photos to reveal the "truth" about the star. The primary goal for celebrity weeklies like *Us Weekly* is to highlight the private persona of the star, thus helping to solidify the star's economic value through attention capital and, importantly, the cultural value of the ideologies embodied by the persona.

Although *Us Weekly* has built its brand on portraying stars as just like us, as discussed in the previous chapter, their attention to celebrity culture remains wrapped in a veneer of extraordinariness, typically defined through attention to stars' glitzy lifestyles rather than appeals to talent. Karen Sternheimer (2011) points out, "Paparazzi shots of celebrities' private lives promote a consumption-based lifestyle, highlighting their expensive clothes, cars, and vacations. Many contemporary fan magazines filled with pictures of celebrities on the red carpet or paparazzi shots of their daily lives are little more than catalogues of advertised goods that we might buy to feel like we are joining their status community" (p. 11). This emphasis on lifestyle points to the ways in which the celebrity is inextricably wrapped up in the American Dream's stories of upward mobility, particularly the "promise to allow [individuals] to rise from obscurity to fame and fortune" (Sternheimer, 2011, p. 1). The traditional myth of stardom rests on the notion that through a mixture of talent, hard work, sheer luck, and the right personality—or that heady mix of creative labor and the labor of ordinariness at the heart of traditional stardom—these individuals have earned their fame and the material wealth that comes with it. The magazines, then, are the vehicles for this justification, elevating stars to a higher status through attention to their glamorous consumption-based lifestyles while simultaneously reminding the reader that they are just like us. In short, they make the extraordinary seem ordinary.

As reality cast members' public performances are already rooted in ordinariness, celebrity weeklies must take a different approach to justify their presence in a *celebrity* magazine. Instead of needing the magazines to humanize the existing celebrity through an appeal to the private self, celebrity weeklies must do the opposite for the reality cast member. They chronicle her celebrity lifestyle labor, inserting her private self into the public realm of glamour as a means to frame her ordinariness as extraordinary and special. This chapter is concerned with this process of celebrification, tracing the contours of how the coverage of reality cast members in *Us Weekly* engages the performance of multiple forms of celebrity lifestyle labor as a means to move these media people rooted in ordinariness into the extraordinariness of celebrity culture. The rise of the reality celebrity in *Us Weekly* is born of the fusion of the labor of ordinariness and celebrity lifestyle labor that creates an extraordinarily ordinary celebrity who is famous for just being herself, but a glamorized version of that self.

Extraordinariness as Promotional Discourse

Celebrities are commodities whose attention capital may be deployed to sell a range of media and cultural products, including, of course, the celebrity herself. Joshua Gamson (1994) makes a distinction between two sorts of "products" that comprise the celebrity commodity: the role as a worker in which "what is sold is the capacity to play a role and the actual work of playing the role" and the role as a celebrity whose value is rooted in "the capacity to attract attention" (p. 58). Historically, the star system emerged as a way to differentiate between films through an appeal to the players, using the attention capital of the featured players as a means to promote the film itself. This is still central to contemporary stardom, as stars begin to make the rounds of talk shows, magazine profiles, and other publicity spaces to promote their latest projects by sharing glimpses of the real person who performed the creative labor. For most celebrities, the creative labor offers the first point of entry into the public eye, and the subsequent promotion of that labor and the media text is an initial mode of celebrity lifestyle labor necessary to move from media person to celebrity. In contrast, as discussed in the previous chapter, reality cast members begin from the labor of ordinariness, or just being yourself, as the point of entry into public purview but still need that appeal to extraordinariness, or the work of celebrity lifestyle labor, to both promote the media text from which they emerge and build and maintain a broader and potentially lasting celebrity image.

The initial attention to reality television cast members in *Us Weekly* primarily functioned in this promotional way, using the attention to the ordinary self who "performed" within the narrative of the reality program to promote that program during its run. For instance, the cover story of the January 29, 2001, issue of *Us Weekly* centered on the second season of *Survivor*, called *Survivor: The Australian Outback*, and offered details of the camp and the challenges and, most importantly, introduced the real cast members to audiences (Papas, 2001, January 29). The focus on the program itself does not explicitly bring these cast members into the glamorous world of stardom—as the conditions of *Survivor* are far from fabulous—and the mini bios included for each cast member center on the details of their ordinary lives before embarking on the challenge of the program. However, it offers that first level of celebrification by helping to familiarize the audience with the cast members as media people who appear on the show and subsequently in other media spaces to promote the show, tightly articulating their public personas to the program itself. Indeed, *Survivor: The Australian Outback* was the primary cover story four times during its 2001 season (January 29, March 12, April 30, and May 21), using the magazine as a vehicle to promote the show through behind-the-scenes access during the season. These articles kept the focus firmly on the contestants' performance of the self within the confines of the program's narrative—offering details on narrative developments, predictions on who would win, and, in the final cover story, an interview with the show's winner and runner-up—thus blurring the lines between creative labor and the labor of ordinariness in the creation of the attention capital of these individuals. As one of the most popular television series of that year, the coverage of *Survivor: The Australian Outback* in *Us Weekly* helped reinforce these ordinary individuals' place in the public eye through their work on the program as themselves. They were media people whose images had some purchase outside of the text of the program, but because, at this point, *Us Weekly* only covered them in the context of the program, they had not yet fully "escaped" into celebrity.

However, the final cover story related to this season appeared in the May 21, 2001, issue, which was available the week after the season finale aired and marked a clear shift from using the cast members' personas to promote the program itself to a promotion of the continued celebrity of (some of) the individuals who emerged from it. The main article kept with the previous show focus by discussing the events of the finale episode that led to Tina Wesson emerging as the winner (Pappas, 2001, May 21a). But a two-page embedded sidebar article attempted to extend her media person status beyond the confines of the program through a discussion of Wesson's personal life and how winning would change it, both through the money she won and the increased opportunity to *be* a celebrity outside of the show (Pappas, 2001, May 21b). A first way Wesson's image was initially separated from the promotion of the program was its use to promote other products, notably a "Got Milk?" advertisement that appeared on the page just prior to these articles. The "Got Milk?" campaign typically features celebrities wearing milk moustaches as a means of promoting dairy products, engaging celebrities' attention capital outside of but often in reference to their creative labor roles. This particular "Got Milk?" ad featured a smiling Wesson with the customary milk moustache reclining in a bubble bath in a gold tub surrounded by works of art and a bottle of milk chilling in a silver dish. The ad copy reads: "After surviving on rice, water and whatever you could catch, enjoying milk's 9 essential nutrients is quite a luxury" (America's Dairy Farmers and Milk Processers, 2001, p. 27). While the nod to luxury here is presented as a winking counterpoint to the decidedly rough conditions Wesson had just endured on *Survivor*, her presence at the center of an ad campaign signals an attempt to use her as a celebrity commodity whose attention capital can be deployed to sell other products outside of the show itself, moving her away from media person and toward celebrity.

It is important at this point to recognize that not all reality cast members become celebrities, and looking at *how* and *which* cast members move from media-person coverage into celebrity coverage in *Us Weekly* reveals the highly feminized and consumerist discourses that shape celebrity lifestyle labor. In fact, winning *Survivor* is itself no guarantee of lasting celebrity, and Wesson quickly faded back into private life after winning season 2. Though the postwin interview with Wesson suggests she was not particularly interested in pursuing the media spotlight after winning *Survivor*, *Us Weekly* was also unlikely to pursue her as a celebrity because she embodied an ordinariness that fell outside of the narrow norms of femininity—specifically youth, beauty, and a focus on romantic relationships/weddings—that are central to its established gossip narrative. Her fellow castaway Elisabeth Filarski (now Hasselbeck), instead, emerged as the real star of the season and is indeed the only member of this cast who successfully parlayed her *Survivor* appearance into a longer-lasting media career (first as a cohost of *The View* from 2002 to 2013 and then cohost of *Fox & Friends* from 2013 to 2015) and position in the category of celebrity. A look at Filarski's post-*Survivor* coverage in *Us Weekly* points to the ways in which the magazine highlights celebrity lifestyle labor as a counterbalance to the ordinary self as both a means to promote the franchise and to build the celebrity status of the reality cast member. In contrast to Wesson, a "40-year-old certified nursing assistant and mother of two," the twenty-three-year-old Filarski was presented in *Us Weekly* as "*Survivor*'s Sweetheart," whose success in the game was tied to her good looks and sunny disposition, or an ordinariness that fit well within the sort of gendered values promoted in the magazine (Papas, 2001, May 21b, pp. 33–34). Consistent with the celebrity's role as a social symbol, being the right kind of ordinary self—that is, a young, white, thin, and conventionally attractive woman—thus becomes a springboard for the performance of celebrity lifestyle labor in *Us Weekly*.

As a finalist, attention to Filarski makes sense as part of the promotional coverage of the show, and an article specifically devoted to Filarski appeared immediately after the one on Wesson in the May 21, 2001, issue. But, in comparison to the piece on Wesson, the tone of the article shifted toward inserting Filarski's properly ordinary image into the feminized discourses that already defined *Us Weekly*'s coverage of celebrity. It paired a glossy glamour shot of Filarski in a bikini—not one taken from the show—with a discussion of her ordinary family life and recent engagement to the football player Tim Hasselbeck, reinforcing the extraordinary/ordinary split and, not coincidentally, the hegemonic norms of femininity recurrent within *Us Weekly*'s coverage of celebrity culture as a means to justify her entrance into that culture. The article continually glamorizes this ordinary person by pointing out that the "dazzling 23-year-old is virtually guaranteed a robust post-*Survivor* string of endorsements," that she was the first *Survivor* contestant to appear on *The Late Show with David Letterman*, and that she is currently deciding on an agent (Papas, 2001, May 21b, p. 35). Her labor here is still tied to the promotion of the program but begins to lay the groundwork to move her persona outside of it: "Less than 36 hours after her red-carpet run [for the finale], Elisabeth is getting the *star treatment* backstage at CBS's Television City, pouring through outfits from the *Hollywood Squares* wardrobe (the *Survivor II* crew will be on the week of May 14) or autographing T-shirts for CBS publicity" (ibid., emphasis mine). The attention to celebrity lifestyle labor—such as appearing on talk shows, wearing high-end clothing, and walking red carpets—serves as a counterbalance to the discussion of the ordinary self, connecting both as part of her image and bypassing the need for creative labor to justify her entrance into the realm of celebrity. Gamson (1994) argues this attention to the individual's "essence" has always been used to bolster fame, saying, "Greatness is built in, it is who you are. If one works at it, or gets a lucky break, it may be discovered. If it is discovered, one becomes celebrated for it, which is evidence that one had it to begin with" (p. 32). The framing of Filarski here suggests that she *already had* the necessary qualities of celebrity, and her appearance on *Survivor* simply offered a springboard for bringing those qualities to the public's attention. She is just being herself but the best type of self that is worthy and able to move outside of the program and more firmly into celebrity culture.

Filarski's celebrification also demonstrates the ways in which the real self at the center of such promotional work is subsumed into claims of glamour and other extraordinary facets of stardom within the pages of *Us Weekly*, or how the ordinary is made extraordinary through celebrity lifestyle labor. For instance, in the lead-up to her appearance on *The Bachelorette*'s third season, Jenn Schefft[1] was included in *Us Weekly*'s regular photo-based feature Faces and Places wearing a beautiful dress and riding in a horse-drawn carriage with a caption suggesting the "new Bachelorette . . . (here, taping a promo in NYC's Central park on October 16) can't wait to shoot her show in the cooler months" (Tomczak, 2004, p. 18). Schefft is presented as ordinary in the photo captions, as she discusses her love of wearing "scarves and great jackets" during the fall months, but readers are also reminded that she is making such fashion choices for when she "shoot[s] the show" (ibid.). This emphasis on femininity and fashion as the work of being a celebrity is intensified in a second photo of Schefft's carriage ride embedded in the first in which the caption notes she is wearing "a Temperly dress from Henri Bendel ($2,708)" and is "followed through the park by extras posing as potential bachelors" while "taping a promo [for the upcoming season] in NYC" (ibid.). *Us Weekly* here explicitly acknowledges that Schefft is doing the professional work we expect of traditional celebrities, such as filming television promos and, more implicitly, being photographed doing so for a celebrity weekly.

Though she performs this labor "as herself," it is framed as glamorous and special by virtue of her designer clothes (price and designer explicitly stated), perfect hair and makeup, and the fact that she, an ordinary person, is filming a promotional spot for a national television program. Thus, while it may appear that she is just being herself or, more disparagingly, doing nothing, *Us Weekly*'s attention to her asserts that the work of promoting a television program in which she appears verifies she is a celebrity.

Entering Celebrity Place

Promotional work offers the reality television cast member an initial step away from the category of media person by taking her outside of the narrative of the program and into what Sue Collins (2008) calls "celebrity place": "the aggregate of media space devoted to celebrity coverage by all facets of the cultural industries. Celebrity place is the seat next to Leno or Letterman, the guest appearance on *Saturday Night Live*, the lead to *Entertainment Tonight*, and the feature story of *People* or *Entertainment Weekly* that function to signify celebrity, symbolically and materially" (p. 101). Though the talk show appearance or the magazine profile is a key space where the labor of ordinariness is engaged, as the celebrity is there to offer controlled glimpses of the real person behind the very performance she is there to promote, the celebrity place is steeped in extraordinariness precisely because ordinary people do not appear as guests on *The Late Show* or on the cover of *Seventeen* or as one of *Maxim*'s annual Hot 100 women. Through the work of promoting the program in these celebrity places, the reality television cast member begins to celebrify her image by simultaneously promoting herself *as* a celebrity because she appears (as herself) in these extraordinary places. *Us Weekly*'s coverage—itself an example of a celebrity place, as will be discussed in more detail below—helps move reality cast members even further away from the reality television program by covering their performance of celebrity lifestyle labor, emphasizing the ways in which these ordinary people are more like other celebrities than they are just like us.

Us Weekly's coverage of reality cast members' appearances in other media forms often works to show how the reality cast member exists alongside known celebrity commodities in these rarified and privileged celebrity places, thus asserting that being in a celebrity place is evidence of celebrity status. This was clear in *Us*'s coverage of the season 1 bachelorette Trista Rehn's appearance on the 2003 *Maxim* Hot 100 list, noting that she "is at No. 7, sharing the list with **Christina Aguilera** and **Shakira**" (Tegnelia & Youngman, 2003, p. 10, emphasis in original). In addition to this explicit positioning of Trista in the company of other established achieved celebrities as the type of extraordinary individuals who would appear on such a list, the accompanying photo offered a behind-the-scenes image from Trista's *Maxim* photo shoot showing her in the act of doing the glamorous promotional work of being a celebrity, much like the previous example of Jenn Schefft filming the promo for *The Bachelorette*. Such coverage serves multiple promotional purposes that benefit the program and celebrifies Trista's image by moving it outside of the program. The most obvious is to use Trista's image, already familiar to the *Us Weekly* reader from coverage of her during her then-recent stint on *The Bachelorette*, to promote the forthcoming *Maxim* issue and the related Hot 100 special that aired on NBC the week the *Us Weekly* issue was released, both of which were explicitly mentioned in the accompanying article. The article also noted the "shoot's concept was a tongue-in-cheek take on a *Bachelorette* white wedding" and made a connection to her upcoming "*real* nuptials, planned for late fall" (ibid., emphasis in original). Here, Trista's celebrity self (as a cast member on *The Bachelorette*) is blurred with the real self who is planning her upcoming wedding, albeit one that was also documented elsewhere in *Us Weekly* and would air as a three-episode miniseries, *Trista & Ryan's Wedding*, on the Disney-owned ABC network the following November and December. Through her public performance of the right sort of heteronormative and hyperfeminine self both within the narrative of *The Bachelorette* and in the pages of *Us Weekly*, the ordinary Trista is brought into the extraordinary realm of celebrity by appearing in another celebrity place alongside other celebrities.

In addition to covering reality television cast members' appearances in other magazines to bolster claims that they are celebrities, *Us Weekly* paradoxically suggests that the fact that these cast members are covered by *Us Weekly* defines them as celebrities. Just as talk shows are celebrity places where we do not see ordinary people, *Us Weekly*'s coverage of traditional celebrities implies that anyone it covers must also be considered a celebrity. Moreover, *Us Weekly* offers *coverage of its own coverage* in an implicit and at times cheeky nod to its own power as an arbiter of celebrity. For example, the season 3 *Bachelor* couple Andrew Firestone and Jenn Schefft were photographed doing the work of being celebrities by appearing at a fan event in June 2003 where, "for six hours, lovebirds Andrew Firestone and Jennifer Schefft signed copies of their *Us* cover and bottles of Firestone wine for over 1,000 fans at Ralph's grocery store in Manhattan Beach, California. 'The store was so packed you couldn't even walk up the aisles!' one attendee marveled to *Us*" (Lipsky-Karasz, 2003, p. 12). Notably, the photos show (and the caption explicitly states) that the couple signed copies of a previous issue of *Us Weekly* featuring them on the cover. Such coverage acknowledges these two are celebrities in part because they previously appeared on the cover of *Us Weekly* and, at the same time, reaffirms the magazine as a purveyor of celebrity culture because it put them on the cover. Similarly, a photo of Heidi Montag on the red carpet at the 2007 Hot Hollywood party showed the *Hills* star holding the copy of the previous week's issue of *Us Weekly* that featured her on the cover (Stars party with *Us*, 2007, October 15, p. 27). Her celebrity is reinforced first by her appearance on a magazine cover—a celebrity place—and second by the fact that the (same) magazine is now covering her red carpet appearance celebrating that appearance.

Working the Red Carpet

While Collins's original definition of celebrity place is specifically tied to more traditional media spaces devoted to celebrity culture, I contend the very celebrity red carpet events themselves, including award shows, film premieres, and the parties held around these and other industry events, also function as celebrity place precisely because they are events steeped in extraordinariness for the specific purpose of being documented by the entertainment-news media. Gamson (1994) posits such events "are consciously and carefully organized to facilitate the capture and dissemination of standardized celebrity images in magazines and on television" (p. 61). The concept of the red carpet calls up ideas of exclusivity and extraordinariness—well-dressed celebrities parading in front of adoring fans, having their photograph taken by paparazzi, and basking in the glow of their own specialness. These events serve multiple and overlapping promotional purposes, drawing attention to the media product through the presence of its stars, reinforcing the place of the star herself within the public's attention, and, of course, selling the conspicuous consumption of the extraordinary celebrity lifestyle. Unlike much of the other coverage of stars in *Us Weekly* that is meant to capture stars unaware and unguarded in their ordinary moments, there is little subterfuge suggesting the red carpet events are anything but staged events in which the stars, as themselves, appear in all their extraordinary glory. That is, we are not meant to think that Brad Pitt just happened to show up at the Oscars in a tuxedo or that Keira Knightly was unknowingly photographed strolling into a movie theater in a designer gown to watch her new film. These glamorous moments are still glimpses, albeit tightly controlled ones, of the real star separate from his or her performing self. They are there in service of their performances but are still themselves—the dazzling and extraordinary selves that justify their deserved fame. Thus, as with the appearances on talk shows or entertainment magazine covers that Collins's original definition references, it is a part of their work as stars to appear at such events *as stars* and thus offer audiences the opportunity to revel in the glamour of celebrity lifestyles. Furthermore, many stars appear at red carpet events, not just those who are directly related to the media product being promoted. Going to and, more importantly, being seen at red carpet events is simply part of the lifestyle labor of celebrities and thus a key space of celebrification for reality television cast members.

Us Weekly features a great deal of coverage of such red carpet events. Major awards shows, such as the Oscars, Emmys, and Grammys, are pillars of the magazine's editorial calendar and are given multiple pages of coverage, detailing who attended the event, what they wore, and other behind-the-scenes details "you didn't see" on the televised broadcasts. The magazine also regularly features photos of stars appearing at a range of industry events, such as film premieres, fashion events, or product launches, as a routine part of their weekly attention to celebrity lifestyles. The point of such coverage is to use celebrity lifestyle labor to reinforce these events as celebrity places and thus remind readers that those who attend such events are, therefore, celebrities. *Us Weekly* occasionally makes this explicit, such as the cheeky captioning photos of the *Joe Millionaire* cast member Evan Marriott's appearances at a film premiere and a Levi's store opening with "Joe Celebrity" (Kozer, 2003, p. 6). This reminds readers that these are, in fact, celebrity places but, as with other coverage of Marriott that will be discussed later in the chapter, sardonically frames his image as that of a celebrity wannabe whose attempt at celebrity lifestyle labor falls short. But most instances are more implicitly framed to amplify celebrity status through appearances in celebrity places, such as when *Us Weekly* covers reality stars at events associated with celebrity culture and alongside traditional achieved celebrities, for example, a photo of the *Keeping Up with the Kardashians* cast member Kim Kardashian attending the Nickelodeon Teen Choice Awards on August 24, 2009, or Lauren Conrad and Audrina Patridge of *The Hills* photographed attending a video game launch party on November 26, 2007 (Burston, 2009; Davis, 2007).

As one of the primary examples of the extraordinarily ordinary celebrity produced within *Us Weekly*, a case study that will be more fully explored in chapter 4, the celebrification of Lauren Conrad, hinges on the magazine's attention to her in these sorts of extraordinary celebrity lifestyle labor contexts while assiduously maintaining her ordinariness at the same time. She is at once an icon of glamour and style for the young female audience to aspire to emulate and a relatable "girl next door" to whom they can feel connected. The extraordinarily ordinary star makes the lifestyle put on display seem attainable, as she is just like us, but also promises an elevated specialness reserved for those who do properly achieve it. For example, in the issue that hit newsstands the week prior to the 2007 MTV Movie Awards, Conrad was featured in the Hot Pics section in a photo box titled "LC's Dress Decision!" in which readers were entreated to "help *The Hills* star choose for the June 3 MTV Movie Awards" (Agresti, 2007, p. 49). The photos showed Lauren trying on three different designer dresses framed by captions noting her thoughts on each dress ("white with a tan is pretty!"), allowing readers to feel like they are shopping with her and sharing this feminized celebrity lifestyle labor of preparing for a red carpet event while simultaneously learning the ropes of being the right sort of feminine self in order to merit public attention. Readers are further brought into the celebrity lifestyle experience through an explicit invitation to vote (via *Us Weekly*'s website) on which dress she should wear to the event. The culmination of this celebrity lifestyle labor occurred when pictures of Lauren on the MTV Movie Awards red carpet wearing the "winning" dress appeared again in the Hot Pics! section in the June 18,

2007, issue alongside photos of more traditional celebrities like the actresses Jessica Alba and Cameron Diaz (MTV Movie Magic! 2007). In the first set of photos, the "ordinary" Lauren prepares to do the glamorous work of being a celebrity, and the reader sees the fruit of this lifestyle labor in the subsequent red carpet photos, thus solidifying her celebrity status through her successful performance of the right sort of glamorous feminine self in the celebrity place of the awards show red carpet.

Appearing at these sorts of events works to celebrify the reality cast member by inserting her into the glitzy lifestyle associated with traditional celebrities and, more importantly, suggesting an equivalence between her and traditional stars through this now shared lifestyle. This is often accomplished through the juxtaposition of visual images of traditional and reality television celebrities in the coverage of celebrity events. The first pages of *Us Weekly*, for instance, always include a Red Carpet photo feature depicting side-by-side images of celebrities at various events, doing "nothing" but the work of looking fabulous at a glitzy event. The photos are typically organized around a fashion-oriented theme, such as "Stylish Black Belts" featuring celebrities wearing white dresses or skirts with black belts (McColgin, 2006, October 2) or "Little White Dresses" featuring celebrities decked out in various "white-hot frocks" (McColgin, 2007, May 7, pp. 6–7). The captions identify the dress designer and the event at which the celebrity was photographed, both of which firmly ensconce the individual within the glamorous lifestyle labor of celebrity. These are not unguarded moments on the street captured by paparazzi photographers but carefully constructed moments of red carpet glamour that support the extraordinary side of celebrity through an appeal to the feminized concerns of fashion and beauty, thus again reinforcing a specific mode of femininity and the feminized labor (the work of "looking good") needed to achieve it as key to the value of these celebrity women.

Sternheimer (2011) argues the photo-heavy nature of glossy celebrity weeklies like "*Us Weekly, Star,* and *Life & Style* . . . are basically product catalogs filled with celebrity models" (p. 233). Traditional achieved stars in their glamorous extraordinary mode have primarily populated *Us Weekly*, but beginning in the mid-2000s, reality stars began to be regularly included as well. Though specific stories about reality celebrities already include style and fashion asides, such as the cyclical discussion of wedding dresses in articles about *Bachelor/Bachelorette* couples or the aforementioned discussion of Jenn Schefft's dress in the Faces and Places section, the inclusion of reality cast members in these more generalized glimpses at Hollywood life is a telling mode of celebrification, as the magazine deems them part of celebrity culture by covering them in the same way it covers traditional stars. For instance, Kristin Cavallari of *The Hills* appeared in both of the previously mentioned Red Carpet features alongside the traditional stars Kerry Washington and Jessica Biel, while her costar Audrina Patridge had an entire Red Carpet photo spread devoted to "Audrina's Mini Marathon" that featured photographs of her wearing minidresses to various red carpet events in October 2009 (Menses, 2009, pp. 2–3). That Audrina appeared as the only celebrity in this particular photo spread, or, more bluntly, without a traditional star to help reinforce her celebrity status, suggests her celebrity lifestyle labor was enough to justify her existence in this celebrity place. Reality stars' appearances at red carpet events are thus a way of entering a celebrity place through the successful performance of a highly gendered mode of celebrity lifestyle labor that fit within the gossip narratives that shape the magazine. The symbiotic relationship between reality celebrity and *Us Weekly* is evident in these moments. The reality cast members are there because they need access to celebrity places and, more crucially, the coverage of them in these places to maintain their celebrity status. *Us Weekly* needs photos, and the more exclusive the better, of stars at events to sell magazines and, at a deeper level, to reinforce the feminized and extraordinary consumption that underscores its framing of celebrity culture.

Perhaps the most obvious example of the ways in which the magazine reinforces the construction of celebrity through lifestyle labor is the appearance of reality stars in the magazine's weekly red carpet fashion feature Who Wore It Best?, a feature purportedly "created" by the editor Janice Min that has been widely copied across the industry (e.g., *In Touch Weekly* and *Life & Style* have both adopted a regular photo feature called Who Wore It Better?) (Min, 2017). Photo features like this position *Us Weekly* as the arbiter of celebrity lifestyle, using the right sort of lifestyle as a means to teach the predominantly female readership what idealized femininity looks like. Who Wore It Best? consists of three or four pairs of photos of celebrities photographed at different red carpet events wearing the same (designer) outfit and rated by "100 people" interviewed by the magazine in celebrity and fashion-oriented public places, such as "L.A.'s Robertson Boulevard" or "NYC's Fifth Avenue." These ratings are then superimposed over the photos, announcing to the reader who really "wore it best" (see fig. 4). No explanations of the different rankings are given, thus encouraging the reader to scrutinize the two images for evidence of what makes one more successful than the other.

This regular photo item almost exclusively features female celebrities, reinforcing Christine Geraghty's (2000) claim that female stars are "particularly likely to be seen as celebrities whose working life is of less interest and worth than their personal life" (p. 196). Who Wore It Best? thus has obvious gendered implications in which female celebrities' primary work is the performance of proper femininity within these celebrity spaces. Who Wore It Best? exemplifies the feminized discourse of fame embraced by *Us Weekly* in which women are valued primarily for their physical appearance, this physical self is subject to close scrutiny for any perceived flaw, and women are in constant and even explicit competition with other women to maintain such valued status. The performative

Figure 4. Who Wore It Best?, February 19, 2007.

nature of femininity—who does it "best"—is implicitly judged and shaped throughout the magazine but is made explicit in these red carpet photo features. In contrast to the professional work of acting, singing, or other creative labor paths to stardom, celebrity lifestyle labor turns the ordinary individual extraordinary by demonstrating successful adherence to the expected gendered glamour of celebrity.

As with other red carpet coverage, Who Wore It Best? also inserts reality stars into celebrity culture through the juxtaposition of these celebrities with more traditional or achieved celebrities, such as a pairing of Audrina Patridge and Lauren Conrad appearing alongside a pairing of the singer Celine Dion and the actress Jessica Alba (McColgin, 2008, April 7, p. 4). That audiences are invited to judge the reality stars (in this case, against each other) in the same way they are invited to judge traditional stars positions reality stars as part of the broader category of celebrity. Who Wore It Best? further reinforces this connection between reality stars and traditional stars by pairing reality cast members against traditional stars as examples of normative femininity in this feature, such as the Who Wore It Best? pairing of Lauren with the *Grey's Anatomy* actress Katherine Heigel on August 4, 2008, or Audrina with the *High School Musical* star Ashley Tisdale on September 24, 2007 (McColgin, 2008, August 4, p. 4; McColgin, 2007, September 24, p. 12). This pairing of reality stars with traditional stars extends beyond the Who Wore It Best? section and into other lifestyle and fashion-oriented features. For example, a section headlined Star Style: Hollywood Trend Watch featured a box dedicated to "Stars Wearing Maxi Dresses" featured paparazzi photographs of the pop singer Gwen Stefani, the actress Hayden Panettiere, the actress Jennifer Love Hewitt, and Lauren Conrad all wearing the trendy fashion, linking all four women together as examples of "Star Style" (Deely, Marchese, McColgin, & Schutte, 2008, p. 84). These stars are framed as equivalent by virtue of their lifestyles and adherence to proper feminine glamour, not through any appeal to talent.

"Hot Hollywood" Parties

Though the constructed nature of red carpet events was never particularly hidden, under Min's editorial leadership *Us Weekly* began to stage its own branded celebrity events as a means to further naturalize the role of celebrity lifestyle labor as part of celebrity culture. The *Us* Hot Hollywood awards—including Hot Young Hollywood (beginning in 2004) highlighting younger and rising stars, Hot Hollywood Style (beginning in 2005) praising celebrities as style and fashion icons, and Hot Hollywood Power Players (beginning in 2007) honoring stars' rising popularity—celebrate winners more in terms of the celebrity lifestyle labor of *being* a celebrity than honoring specific efforts of creative labor. These are not the Oscars or Emmys, which ostensibly honor a superlative creative performance. Rather, they are a means for *Us Weekly* to highlight individuals they think are "hot" at the moment, bestowing accolades on those who do the work of *being* a celebrity well. As with coverage of other awards shows, *Us Weekly*'s coverage of the Hot Hollywood awards includes copious photos of and insider access to the parties at which the honorees are feted. Essentially, the various Hot Hollywood awards are simply an opportunity for *Us Weekly* to throw a celebrity-studded Hollywood party that can then be exclusively covered in the pages of the magazine to highlight the glamour of celebrity lifestyles. Such managed coverage of celebrity lifestyle labor helps stars of all types maintain their position within the extraordinary realm of celebrity culture and reinforce *Us Weekly*'s role as an important celebrity place. The May 11, 2009, issue featured a two-page photo spread titled "A Night Out with *Us*!" highlighting the red carpet appearances of achieved celebrities, such as the actress Taraji P. Henson, the country singer Martina McBride, and "2009's Style Icon" pop singer Fergie at the *Us*-hosted Hot Hollywood Style event (pp. 18–19). The event explicitly highlighted the glamorous lifestyle labor of (mainly female) celebrities as evidence of their extraordinary status. Reality cast members, in this case Lauren Conrad, Melissa Rycroft (*The Bachelor*), and Kara DioGuardi (*American Idol*), were also featured alongside these traditional stars in this celebrity place, thus reinforcing their status as celebrities because *Us Weekly* says they are and, crucially, provides evidence of their celebrity lifestyle labor that proves it.

Extraordinary Life Events

As seen in the previous chapter, coverage of celebrities' private lives in celebrity media like *Us Weekly* emphasizes their ordinariness as an important humanizing counterbalance to the extraordinary side of stardom that makes celebrities and the ideologies they embody relatable to audiences. As Andrea McDonnell (2014) argues, through this appeal to ordinariness in celebrity gossip magazines, female celebrities, in particular, "become part of our extended family, not only by virtue of their age and gender, but because their experiences are presented as typical, understandable, and shared" (pp. 64–65). But this ordinariness is often wrapped in the sheen of specialness, as the lives the stars lead are like ours but a more glossy and glamorous version. Indeed, in defining traditional stardom, Dyer (1998) argues, "The way stars lived is one element in the 'fabulousness' of Hollywood," asserting that the existence within the celebrity culture (e.g., "Hollywood") is ontologically distinct from living in the "real world" (p. 35). Stars may pick up their kids from school just like us, but they pick them up from exclusive schools while wearing designer clothes and driving luxury vehicles (and while being photographed by paparazzi). The inextricable tie between celebrity and consumer cultures reminds audiences that celebrities are special and offers an aspirational path to that specialness through discourses on lifestyle. That is, readers may not be on television or in films, like the celebrities in the magazine, but they can live the same lifestyle through the purchase of the luxury products that shape the fabulous lives of stars. Accordingly, the performance of celebrity lifestyle labor in *Us Weekly* also takes a form in which the work of *being* a celebrity is about the extraordinary ways celebrities live out the milestones of contemporary life.

In addition to the more obviously staged promotional events discussed above, *Us Weekly* routinely uses reality television cast members in narratives of extraordinary life events as a means to celebrify them. By life events, I mean such milestones in an individual's life as an engagement, a wedding, or the birth of a child that move beyond the quotidian events of everyday life that typically comprise the labor of ordinariness discussed in the previous chapter. These life events are the sorts of more significant moments in an ordinary person's life that are, within the pages of *Us Weekly*, even *more* extraordinary when they happen to celebrities, helping to intensify the celebrity self as a symbol of social success. The sorts of life events focused on in the magazine are framed through a heteronormative lens that reinforces to the young female readership that marriage and children are women's ultimate goal. Furthermore, achieving such life events is also tied to the proper consumption of consumer goods, connecting the performance of successful femininity and conspicuous consumption to celebrity status. Importantly, these life events are not read as explicitly staged simply for coverage in the magazine in the same way red carpet events are. The articles, with their staged photos rather than paparazzi shots and more carefully managed interviews, certainly bear the marks of media construction, but readers are not generally encouraged to think a celebrity gets married or has a child *just* for the media attention. *Us Weekly*'s cheeky yet loving approach to celebrity may challenge celebrity images at times, but such a cynical view is not generally invited in the magazine because such constructed moments are counterbalanced with the appeals to the ordinary and authentic self. In other words, the life event is real and relatable, while the fabulous way the celebrity lives it *and* the magazine's coverage of it elevate it to the level of extraordinary. By essentially transforming these life events and the successful gendered performance of them into celebrity places, *Us Weekly* reinforces the specialness of celebrities and, particularly in the case of their coverage of reality television cast members, uses this specialness to further insert them into celebrity culture.

Celebrity Weddings

Perhaps the pinnacle of extraordinary life events in *Us Weekly* is the celebrity wedding, which offers a potent symbol of feminine success in achieving a heteronormative coupling marked by the "perfect wedding." Given the underlying appeal to ordinariness—as these are life events that dominant culture suggests all women are allegedly inclined to pursue—the reality cast member can use these sorts of events to maintain or bolster her place in celebrity culture by performing them in an extraordinary way. For instance, since the premise of *The Bachelor/Bachelorette* is that the cast member will find his or her one true love through the course of the program, *Us Weekly*'s coverage of each season's winning couple's relationship after the program ends keeps the ordinary self at the heart of their images while simultaneously inserting them into celebrity culture through appeals to the glamorous and extraordinary performance of these life events. In short, these life events are opportunities for ordinary reality cast members to become extraordinary through the performance of the conspicuous consumption that underscores celebrity lifestyle labor.

The cover story of the September 8, 2003, issue proclaimed "Trista and Ryan Talk: Our Dream Wedding Details! Gowns, Flowers & More: The Couple Reveal All Their Big Day Plans." Coverage of celebrity weddings is a mainstay for *Us Weekly*, and including the *Bachelorette* couple in such coverage is a first means of taking these reality cast members out of the specific narrative confines of the program and inserting them into the glamorous world of celebrity culture. The cover story highlighted the extraordinary nature of their wedding—an event far more luxurious and glamorous than the average reader would be able to afford—and directly compared them to the over-the-top celebrity weddings of Gwen Stefani and Gavin Rossdale and Jennifer Aniston and Brad Pitt in an article insert (Bartolomeo, 2003, September 8, p. 46). It detailed Trista's work with a high-end designer on not one but two dresses for the wedding and placed a pull quote indicating her hope that the jewelry designer to the stars Harry Winston, "who did her 1½ caret engagement ring" will "take care of" the wedding jewelry alongside a photo of $98,000 diamond and platinum drop earrings designed by the jeweler (p. 47). This cover story was followed by an article in the November 10, 2003, issue detailing "Trista's Wedding Dress Dreams" in which a "virtual dressing room" allowed readers to see what Trista would look like wearing four different wedding gowns by the high-end designer Badgley Mischka by Photoshopping her into them. These Photoshopped images highlighted Trista as a celebrity commodity whose body could be traded between high-end wedding gowns in order to emphasize the glamorous choice she faced as a celebrity bride-to-be. The article also included behind-the-scenes photos of Trista being primped for her photo shoot for the July 18 cover of *Modern Bride* (itself a celebrifying move, as previously discussed) in which she "had 30 gowns to choose from" (Ratledge, 2003, November 10, pp. 52–53). Throughout this consumption-based coverage, Trista's wedding is framed as equivalent to the "fabulousness" of celebrity weddings even though she is an ordinary individual.

Though Trista and Ryan were the first *Bachelor/Bachelorette*-produced couple to actually wed and one of only two during the first ten years of the programs' existence to do so, the attention to their wedding extends the cyclical celetoid mode of *Bachelor* coverage through an appeal to celebrity lifestyle labor, as most *Bachelor/Bachelorette* couples routinely discussed as "engaged" or "planning a wedding" as part of their postfinale coverage. Even the celetoid-level status of these reality celebrities, then, is already tied to the extraordinary glamour and consumption of a celebrity wedding. For example, after appearing in the typical postfinale interview on March 15, 2004, the season 2 bachelorette, Meredith Phillips, was featured in an "*Us* Exclusive" article titled "Meredith's Wedding Dress" on June 21, 2004, which detailed her search for a dress and included sketches of dresses designed exclusively for her by several high-end designers (Bartolomeo,

2004, June 21, pp. 68–69). Similarly, an insert in an article about the breakup of the season 12 couple, Matt Grant and Shayne Lamas, reminded readers that other cast members were still living out the heteronormative fantasy of the show by showing the season 4 bachelorette, DeAnna Pappas, trying on high-end wedding gowns at "L.A.'s Monique Lhuiller boutique" as part of planning her wedding to the "winner" Jesse Csincsak (Davis, 2008, p. 67). Neither of these weddings took place (and, of course, their breakups were also covered by the magazine), but the extraordinariness that surrounded the coverage of these life events helped extend these cyclical celetoids' life cycle in celebrity culture through the work of conspicuous consumption that underscores celebrity lifestyle labor.

The emphasis on conspicuous consumption as a form of lifestyle labor was essential to moving the reality cast member beyond cyclical celetoid status and growing a more lasting extraordinarily ordinary celebrity. Trista and Ryan, as previously stated, were the first and one of the few *Bachelor/Bachelorette* couples to wed and were also the first to do so in front of reality television cameras. The wedding was the culmination of their *Bachelorette* narrative, as the premise of the show rests on cast members finding "true love," thus the wedding was an important vehicle for catapulting their (particularly Trista's) images out of the narrative of the program and into broader celebrity culture. Their wedding ceremony, which was broadcast on ABC on December 10, 2003, and covered in the December 22, 2003, issue of *Us Weekly*, was an opulent affair steeped in the glamour and fabulousness of celebrity lifestyle labor. *Us Weekly*'s coverage highlighted the extravagance of the event, noting the bride wore a "$20,000 Badgley Mischka gown" for the ceremony and then donned a second designer gown for the reception, where the guests dined on "porcini-and-spinach ravioli, swordfish confit or filet mignon" (Reinstein, 2003, December 22, pp. 54–55). As a televised special, the wedding took on an extra air of celebrity fabulousness, as even though Trista and Ryan were continually framed as ordinary people through the underlying discourses of authenticity that shape reality television, most ordinary people do not have $4 million weddings broadcast on national television.

Us Weekly's coverage of other reality cast members' weddings similarly frames the conspicuous consumption of this life event as evidence of the move from media person to celebrity. For example, the *Survivor* cast members Rob Mariano and Amber Brkich's[2] engagement and wedding received attention in the magazine, though far less than Trista and Ryan's, likely, in part, because of Rob and Amber's tie to CBS, a competing media conglomerate. Nevertheless, the centrality of the celebrity wedding as an aspirational discourse in *Us Weekly* and the ease in which ordinary reality cast members can be inserted into the realm of extraordinariness through narratives of consumption meant Rob and Amber's wedding was still an extraordinary life event worthy of coverage by the magazine.

Rob and Amber did not appear as the main focus of any *Us Weekly* covers, but their "Dream Wedding" did warrant a second-level cover story in the May 30,

2005, issue. This article explicitly functioned as a "preview of the two-hour CBS special where *Survivor/Amazing Race* sweeties Rob Mariano and Amber Brkich say 'I do'" (Reinstein, 2005, p. 56). The article highlighted their ordinariness through a discussion of their comparatively, by celebrity standards, low-key destination wedding on a beach in the Bahamas but noted it was paid for by CBS and quoted Amber as saying, "[We did it] for the money," in an explicit reveal of the economic rewards attached to performing such lifestyle labor (p. 58). Nevertheless, this nod to celebrity lifestyle—as most ordinary people do not get their weddings paid for by and aired on a major national television network—was bolstered by the two large photos of the couple during a *Modern Bride* photo shoot featuring Amber in designer wedding dresses. The captions plainly stated these photos were from that shoot, not the wedding, and provided the name of the designer and price of each dress. Even as the more ordinary narrative of their relationship and comparatively less extravagant wedding functioned as the core of the story, the photos worked to reaffirm the extraordinariness of celebrity weddings and mark these two as part of the celebrity world through two modes of celebrity lifestyle labor: conspicuous consumption and doing magazine photo shoots. To further solidify their extraordinariness, a photo of the couple's Bahamian wedding was included in a two-page photo spread in the July 25, 2005, issue style feature "Where Other Stars Wed" next to Renée Zellweger and Kenny Chesney (Where other stars wed, 2005, July 25, p. 68). By explicitly juxtaposing the reality celebrities to the "other" achieved celebrities, the magazine solidifies their position within celebrity culture and, not coincidentally, reinforces the importance of conspicuous consumption around these life events for the average reader.

Fame Damage: Changed by Celebrity

In *Us Weekly*, the notion of celebrity as something extraordinary is further reinforced through narratives of how the once ordinary individual's life is changed when he or she becomes a celebrity. Celebrity lifestyle labor is evidence of this change because it is rooted in access to celebrity places and the fabulous consumer lifestyle of the rich and famous. Yet beneath the aspirational narratives of celebrity culture runs a question of merit in which celebrities are judged for "deserving" the lifestyle and attention they are afforded. Without a claim to talent to buoy the image, the reality star must perform a careful balancing act between ordinary and extraordinary to prove she deserves celebrity status and the lifestyle that comes with it. While much of the coverage in *Us Weekly* celebrates the entrance of the ordinary reality cast member into the fabulous and extraordinary realm of celebrity, it also consistently reminds audiences of the importance of that authentic and ordinary core to the reality celebrity's image. In other words, the reality star cannot *only* perform lifestyle labor. It must be seen as earned through the continued claim of authenticity and ordinariness that brought the individual into the public eye in the first place. We see a glimpse of this in the Rob and Amber wedding coverage, as Amber's sardonic claim that they did it "for the money" reconnects them with the noncelebrity reader, who may struggle to afford her dream wedding, while simultaneously stressing the cultural importance of having a more lavish wedding. Tying the earned celebrity lifestyle with a consistent appeal to authentic ordinariness makes a reality television celebrity a potent social symbol of success in which only the right kind of person deserves fame and others are mocked as false celebrities.

Us Weekly's initial coverage of *Survivor*'s first season in 2000 focused primarily on the show itself during the broadcast run but quickly moved to insert several of the cast members into the broader celebrity culture through an appeal to lifestyle labor after the winner, Richard Hatch, was announced. Hatch was the first ever reality show winner to be featured on the cover of the magazine, on September 18, 2000,[3] and the cover's headline, "Surviving *Survivor*: How Fame and Money Are Changing Their Lives," explicitly framed him *as* a celebrity because of his newfound access to an extraordinary lifestyle. The story focused on the private lives of the cast members, emphasizing how their once ordinary lives changed by virtue of participation on the show. They were not simply media people here; rather, the focus on what happened to them after and outside of the narrative of the show reinforced them as newfound celebrities. Though the cover story was primarily an interview with Hatch, all of the season's cast members were discussed first in terms of attempts to legitimate their stardom by securing work within the media industry, such as Rudy Bosch's upcoming appearance on the CBS drama *JAG* or Gervase Peterson's gigs as an *Access Hollywood* correspondent or guest spots on the comedy *The Hughleys* (Pappas, 2000). Similarly, Hatch was discussed as fielding "countless offers" and, in a clear move into the circuit of celebrity production, hiring "people," including "a lecture agent, a book agent, a manager, a publicist and a talent agent at Creative Artists Agency, which also represents Will Smith and Tom Cruise" (p. 55). Consistent with celebrity culture's myth of meritocracy, the rhetoric of this story suggests the reality show here provided the "lucky break" for the real talents of these ordinary individuals to be discovered by virtue of the public visibility the show offered. Additionally, since the show had already presented the authentic and real individuals, they could be inserted into the machinery of celebrity culture because despite the artifice and control of the image within its inner workings, the audience could rest assured these stars were still, at the core, the same ordinary self seen on the reality program.

The appeal to (potential) creative labor helps anchor the image in the possibility of extended visibility, but Hatch's and the other cast members' real status as celebrities in *Us Weekly* was primarily framed through their newfound access to celebrity places and the ability to successfully perform celebrity lifestyle labor within them. In the article, Hatch discussed his plans to install "a 12-person Jacuzzi" in his backyard and his attempts to purchase land from neighbors on either side of his home to "increase his privacy" in the wake of his newfound celebrity (Pappas, 2000, p. 56). An insert within the larger article on Hatch focused on his fellow castaway Sean Kenniff and the perks of his fame: jumping the line at an exclusive club "favored by Leonardo DiCaprio, Jennifer Lopez and Puff Daddy," having a stylist "arrange for him to borrow an $8,000 Dolce & Gabbana suit to wear to the *Survivor* finale party at the Mondrain hotel's Skybar in Los Angeles," and chatting with adoring fans (p. 58–59). The article self-consciously reinforced the ordinariness of both Hatch and Kenniff, stressing how they were outsiders new to this world of fame and therefore retain their authentic ordinary selves. Hatch, for example, was described as "surprised" at the attention from fans, saying, "It's like I'm some bird!" (p. 56). Kenniff, similarly, was described as actively returning some of the many phone calls he received from fans on his publicly listed phone number: "I chat with anyone who [gets me] because I'm very flattered that they would call" (p. 59). The article ultimately claims these two reality celebrities retain their ordinary appeal and thus deserve the celebrity status earned through the related performance of celebrity lifestyle labor.

Not all who perform celebrity lifestyle labor are framed as worthy of such fame, however. Dyer (1998) says, "Stars can be seen as ordinary people who live more expensively than the rest of us but are not essentially transformed by this" (p. 43). Access to extraordinary lifestyles is evidence of the social mobility and material abundance promised by both celebrity status and the American Dream but also serves to reinforce norms about who is truly deserving of that dream. In keeping with the myth of meritocracy, it is only those ordinary individuals who reinforce the Puritan work ethic and sense of self-control and proper taste in consumption who deserve to be among the celebrity elite. This is particularly true for reality stars precisely because their stardom remains tied to their ordinariness even as they enter the celebrity place of extraordinary lifestyles. The reality celebrity can enjoy the spoils of celebrity lifestyles, but she must not be spoiled *by* them. Failure in this regard does not mean the star necessarily disappears from the public eye, as star images have long served a role as cautionary morality tales of "lifestyle of excess and moral failure and serve as ready-made whipping boys for class-based animosity" (Sternheimer, 2011, p. 13). The failings of reality celebrities, in particular, serve to bolster the importance of talent and/or authenticity as the core of celebrity, reaffirming the idea of hard work inherent to the mythos of the American Dream as well as the pecking order of fame that valorizes achieved celebrities as the pinnacle of deserved and, therefore, righteous fame.

In some cases, *Us Weekly* uses reality cast members' existence (or attempted existence) within the extraordinary world of celebrity to reinforce narratives of celebrity as a corrosive influence on the ordinary self. If a reality cast member is *too* changed by entrance into the celebrity world, his or her celebrity status is read as damaged. This may discredit the reality celebrity in question, but it simultaneously serves to reinforce the deserved celebrity status of other celebrities, including other reality cast members who, like the previously discussed examples of Trista (Rehn) Sutter or Elisabeth Filarski (Hasselbeck), successfully balance their celebrity lifestyle labor with a continued sense of authenticity. In contrast, the *Joe Millionaire* cast member Evan Marriott's brief celebrity arc within *Us Weekly* provides an instructive example about the importance of authenticity to the reality celebrity's image and the potential threat the improper performance of celebrity lifestyle labor presents to it. Marriott was the titular "Joe Millionaire" on the first season of the *Bachelor*-style dating competition with the twist that the women competing for his affection believed him to be a millionaire (having purportedly recently inherited $50 million) when he was a working-class construction worker from Florida. The audience was in on the ruse from the beginning, and the pleasures of the show were rooted in seeing if the women were interested in Marriott for his real self or for his (nonexistent) fortune and whether the winner would choose to stay with him when the truth was revealed. The show was wildly popular with a reported forty million viewers tuning in to Fox for the final episode on February 17, 2003 (Levin, 2003). Such public visibility certainly offered a first level of entry to celebrity status for Marriott (as well as to the two finalists, Sarah Kozer and Zora Andrich) by framing them as media people. However, even though the show was premised on the idea that women were supposed to fall for the real Marriott instead of his nonexistent money, the fakery involved in the narrative bled over into his attempts to translate his ordinary self into the extraordinary world of celebrity.

The appeals to ordinariness were present in the early coverage of Marriott in *Us Weekly*. He was featured on the cover of the January 27, 2003, issue, which promised an "exclusive" interview that would reveal the "truth about the phony $50 million heir . . . and how the duped women feel now." At this point, fakery and inauthenticity were already framed as part of his image, even as the interview attempted to show him as an average and real guy. He appeared as a second-level cover story on the February 24 issue (which, given the magazine publishing schedule, would have had an on-sale date of February 14, three days before the finale), accompanying a story billed as "Inside the Tense Final Catfight" that speculated on the finale's outcome but focused mostly on interviews with the final two female contestants. He appeared as a second-level cover story again on the March 31, 2003, issue when he and the winner Zora Aldrich "called it quits," and it is here that claims of his inauthenticity became more prevalent. In the story, Aldrich states that Marriott was "so caught up in everything. I'd rather be with a construction worker than someone who craves the spotlight like that" (Tegnelia, 2003, p. 32). Interest in him as a celebrity was largely thwarted by inappropriate efforts at celebrity image rooted primarily in lifestyle labor instead of a maintenance of his real self outside of the narrative of the show.

Marriott did appear two different times in the Love Lives section (on May 5 and July 21, 2003) with photos and brief details about the (noncelebrity) women he was dating at the time, but *Us Weekly* showed little interest in detailing his personal life after the show—and his relationship with Aldrich—ended. Overall, his attempts to enter the extraordinary level of celebrity, whether through lifestyle labor of appearing at industry events or even acquiring other creative labor work, were met with a cool reception in the pages of *Us Weekly*, which framed him as a mere celetoid. A short one-page article that was mostly dominated by a photo from July 7, 2003, mockingly titled "Evan's 16th Minute of Fame," detailed Marriott's attempts to secure work as an actor, though mostly in cameo appearances as himself or on the "low-budget comedy *Miss Castaway*," suggesting he had already overstayed his welcome in celebrity culture (Ratledge, July 7–14, p. 6). It may be the case that a male star, unlike a female star, is less closely tied to the lifestyle labor of fashion and beauty or the gendered attention to weddings and relationships typical of *Us Weekly*'s coverage of reality celebrities and is therefore less likely to be elevated to celebrity status via lifestyle labor. Indeed, *Us Weekly*'s editor in chief Janice Min (2017) said of the magazine's stories, "The protagonists of every story had to be female. No male point of view was allowed. Kiss of death? A solo male cover." Without the tie to the women and romantic relationships created on *Joe Millionaire*, Marriott had little to offer in terms of attracting the desired female readership. Furthermore, that the very concept of ordinariness was always under threat in Marriott's image, given its origins in the false pretenses of the show, his attempts at solo fame only further damaged his celebrity potential.

Other reality stars have also had their images damaged by claims of being "fame whores" or trying too hard to achieve fame for fame's sake via lifestyle labor rather than because they deserved it. Kristin Cavallari, who first emerged as the star of *Laguna Beach* and joined the cast of its spin-off show *The Hills* in 2009 after Lauren Conrad's departure, was frequently framed as a fame whore whose machinations to insert herself more deeply into celebrity culture via lifestyle labor were evidence of an inauthentic self spoiled by and therefore underserving of celebrity status. An October 12, 2009, article detailing her position as the new star of *The Hills* suggested Cavallari returned to reality television for the money in the wake of a failed attempt to parlay her original reality celebrity into creative work as an actress and because "says a source, 'it killed her to watch Lauren become more and more famous. She sees [the return to reality television] as the chance to create *The Kristin Show*'" (Souter, 2009, p. 66). This article appeared next to a photo of Cavallari "coz[ying] up to Katy Perry at the VMAs" in a juxtaposition that suggests her presence in the celebrity place of red carpet celebrity events is not authentic but manipulated for the sake of undeserved and unearned fame (ibid.).

Of course, such events and stories are, as previously discussed, carefully staged to help promote celebrity, but it is important that they not *look* like they are. After a March 27, 2006, article alleged that Cavallari had begun secretly dating the former boy-band member turned solo singer Nick Lachey, who had recently and publicly split with pop star wife Jessica Simpson,[4] as a "fame shortcut," with Cavallari feeding details of her private life to the press in exchange for publicity: "Even the singer himself became suspicious of the starlet's motivations, says [a Lachey pal], after details of their encounters went public. 'People warned him, but he gave her the benefit of the doubt," the friend tells *Us*. 'Then all these stories started coming out and the details were accurate, so he knows it had to have come from her'" (O'Leary, 2006, pp. 52–53). The implication is that Cavallari's interest in Lachey was not authentic but was instead about generating publicity for herself via the lifestyle labor of a high-profile celebrity romance, thus framing her as desperate and fake. *Us* further reinforced the notion of deserved versus undeserved fame by explicitly comparing Cavallari to Lachey's ex, Jessica Simpson, and suggesting that Cavallari was deliberately copying her lifestyle labor in an attempt to replicate Simpson's deserved fame. An article in the following week's issue focused on Lachey's "autobiographical new video" about the pain of his breakup with Simpson included a nearly two-page side box insert titled "Is Kristin Stealing Jessica's Poses?" in which photos of Cavallari at red carpet events holding the same pose or facial expression as Simpson were evaluated by a "body language expert" as examples of "red carpet copycatting," and Cavallari's attempts were found to be forced and inauthentic in comparison to Simpson's (McColgin, 2006, April 3, p. 56–57). Cavallari was "still copying Jess!" two weeks later, according to an article offering more comparisons of red carpet body language (Abrahamson, 2006 p. 38). This narrative reaffirmed the hierarchy of fame by framing Simpson as the real celebrity and Cavallari as a publicity-hungry wannabe who was trying to acquire undeserved fame by copying her. For the reality celebrity, the performance of celebrity lifestyle labor is key to their existence within celebrity space, but it must be buoyed by an appeal to the authentically real ordinary self that brought them to the public's attention in the first place in order to stay there.

Fame damage is not simply about how an ordinary individual connives to achieve fame, but it is also about how fame can destroy the ordinary person and the norms she is meant to embody. In perhaps the most dominant fame damage story of the time period, *Us Weekly* devoted an unprecedented seven main cover stories in a row between May 11 and June 22, 2009 (with an additional five second-level cover stories and two primary cover stories appearing between July 6 and October 19, 2009), to the infidelity and divorce scandals surrounding Kate and

Jon Gosselin, the stars of the TLC docu-soap *Jon & Kate Plus 8* that documented their lives as parents to a set of twins and a set of sextuplets. This sudden explosion in public interest in the Gosselins speaks to Janice Min's instinct for "see[ing] the potential in stories, in people . . . that other people don't see and elevating" those stories into the public consciousness (Sharpe, 2017). The former *Us Weekly* deputy managing editor Amy Vinciguerra recalls Min saying:

> "That dad of eight on that little show on TLC is cheating on his wife. Would that make you care about the show?" And I said to Janice "yeah, wait, he's cheating on her? With who? Wait a minute, hold on . . . eight kids and he's cheating?!" And then we had a stringer number of I think it was eight consecutive over a million sales. So a million copies in a week, eight consecutive.[5] And I would have friends say to me "Please stop putting Jon and Kate on the cover." And I'd have to say "please stop buying it" . . . We broke [the cheating scandal] at a time when most people had never heard of Jon and Kate. Now they wish they had never heard of Jon and Kate. That's the impact of *Us*. (ibid.)

This "summer of the Gosselins" certainly elevated these two, particularly Kate, as most of the coverage centered on her, to a greater level of fame by increasing their public visibility well beyond their middling cable reality television program. The show, which previously averaged around 2.5 million viewers per week, drew 9.8 million viewers to the May 25, 2009, season 5 premiere and 10.7 million viewers to the June 22, 2009, episode in which the couple announced their separation (Crupi, 2009, June 29). However, the show quickly returned to its typical audience numbers and, after being renamed *Kate Plus 8* in the wake of the divorce, was canceled in 2011 (though briefly revived from 2015 to 2017 for two short, six-episode seasons) (ibid.).

Us Weekly was initially a sympathetic vehicle for Kate, as the magazine's coverage was centered on how she weathered the storm of her husband's affair and the couple's subsequent divorce. However, as the scandal continued, Kate's image quickly turned into one marked by fame damage that was decidedly *not* the sort of identity readers were meant to identify with and strive to emulate. In contrast to the earlier softening of her image in the wake of the cheating scandal, *Us Weekly*'s later narratives intensified Kate's domineering maternal presence on *Jon & Kate Plus 8* and framed her as a "mean mommy" who pushed her husband to cheat and used her family for fame. This view of her damaged ordinary self not only prohibited Kate from developing an image rooted in performing the right sort of identity; it also barred her from using celebrity lifestyle labor as a means to maintain celebrity status. Indeed, *Us Weekly* framed any such work as a cautionary tale of how fame damaged her real self. The June 1, 2009, cover story was titled "From Mom . . . to Monster" and promised readers details of a the formerly "relatable stay-at-home mom . . . who has fallen in love with fame and fortune at the expense of almost all else (Reinstein & Sóuter, 2009, p. 66).

The article details the amount of money Kate routinely spends on shoes, cosmetic procedures, tanning, and nails (ibid.). But instead of framing this as aspirational, as in the wedding-planning coverage discussed earlier, Kate's celebrity lifestyle labor is "disturbing" and "diva behavior" done at the expense of her responsibilities to her family as well as her fans, who the article points out are charged "up to $150 per ticket" on her book tour (pp. 66–67). Kate is not extraordinarily ordinary; rather, she embodies the potential damage of fame not only to oneself but to one's children. She has sacrificed her authenticity and true value as a wife and mother and thus does not deserve the spoils of celebrity. But scandals have a shelf life, and thus so too does the reality celebrity whose fame depends on them. Since the dust settled on her divorce, Kate Gosselin has not appeared on another cover of *Us Weekly*, and her fame has been largely diminished in general. She certainly has some fans and remains in the public eye, but her *Us Weekly* fame (or infamy) ended when her image could no longer earn profits for the magazine.

Celebrity Lifestyle Labor and Extraordinary Ordinariness

Traditional definitions of stardom underscore the contrast between the extraordinary performing self, typically sustained by claims to talent, and the offstage, or ordinary, self. Through the negotiation of these "complex and contradictory" categories, stars function as potent images of identity, articulating "aspects of living in contemporary society" (Dyer, 1986, p. 8). Stars, then, represent the best—or the worst—of "what it is to be a human being in contemporary society" (ibid.). Yet the traditional grounding of stardom within a claim to talent or skill has been displaced in contemporary culture, as increasing attention to the private lives of these public figures across celebrity media promotes the ordinary and real self as the core of the image. Reality celebrities, while not the only example of this increasing focus on the private self, offer unique insight into this contemporary shift from star to celebrity. Their entrance into the circuit of celebrity production is predicated on ordinariness, or just being themselves, within the confines of reality television. Yet once brought into that circuit, this ordinariness must, in some ways, be transformed into extraordinariness to justify and maintain their place within the lofty status of celebrity. That is, coverage of the real lives of these reality cast members outside of the narrative confines of the reality program are necessarily framed through the same appeals to the glamorous lifestyles that already define a feminized and consumerist celebrity culture. Reality celebrities are still being themselves, but that self is now framed through the extraordinary and dazzling work of being a celebrity.

Such lifestyle labor is at the heart of contemporary celebrity culture, and reality celebrities make particularly potent symbols precisely because of their ordinary origins. By showcasing how the ordinary individual can enter the extraordinary world of celebrity by simply being herself, celebrity media reinforces the heteronormative and consumerist ideologies that underscore dominant culture. In other words, only by being the right kind of self can the reality cast member enter and remain within the world of celebrity culture. The emphasis on such feminine concerns as fashion, beauty, relationships, and domestic life within such magazines as *Us Weekly* reinforces these dominant norms to the predominantly female audience and makes them seem attainable by attaching them to the reality cast member, who is always already ordinary and just like us. The most successful reality celebrities are able to connect this performance of celebrity lifestyle labor to the ordinary self, seamlessly blending the ordinary with the extraordinary in the pages of *Us Weekly*. The next chapter will explore *Us Weekly*'s construction of celebrity around the women of *The Hills*, most notably Lauren Conrad, through a negotiation of both the private and ordinary selves displayed within the confines of the program's narrative and the extraordinary performance of celebrity lifestyle labor outside of it.

CHAPTER 4

LAUREN CONRAD

US WEEKLY AND THE EXTRAORDINARILY ORDINARY CELEBRITY

Under the continued direction of its editor in chief, Janice Min, and her proven ability to "not only capture the zeitgeist of the moment" but drive celebrity culture with the celebrities and stories she chose to cover in the magazine, *Us Weekly* was riding high in the first half of the decade (Sharpe, 2017). The title "reported an average paid and verified circulation of 1.75 million over the second half of 2006, up 5% from second-half 2005" (Ives, 2007, February 12, p. 4). The *New York Times* media reporter Richard Pérez-Peña (2008) affirmed that *Us Weekly* grew its circulation an additional 10 percent between 2006 and 2007, "despite an increase in its newsstand price last fall" (para. 3). As a result of this success, Wenner Media borrowed heavily to regain full control of the magazine, buying back the 50 percent stake it sold to the Walt Disney Corporation in August 2006 at a price tag of $300 million, compared to the $40 million Disney paid for it back in 2001 (The week, 2006). The average reader likely did not even register this corporate exchange, as little changed after the sale. The editor in chief, Janice Min, remained in place and continued the successful formula that had driven *Us Weekly* to the top of the celebrity weekly market in the early part of the decade.

However, this reacquisition was a crucial business move for Wenner Media, given the massive success of the magazine in the first half of the decade. In fact, Min claims *Us Weekly* was "the ATM" for Wenner Media, accounting for around 70 percent of the company's total revenue and, subsequently, helping to keep more "legitimate" titles, such as Jann Wenner's beloved *Rolling Stone*, afloat (WNYC Studios, 2018; Kelly, 2014). But Wenner Media's decision to go into debt to reacquire the crown jewel of the celebrity weekly market quickly bumped up against the 2008 economic recession and a stagnating print media market. As the decade progressed, magazine subscription and newsstand sales stalled across the industry. According to the Audit Bureau of Circulations report for the second half of 2007, the formerly booming niche of celebrity weeklies was in decline, with titles like *Star* down 4.1 percent and *Life & Style Weekly* down 9.67 percent in terms of single issue newsstand sales (Stableford, 2008). Even *Us Weekly*'s exceptional growth rate was slowing from its earlier peak, with circulation increasing just under 7 percent in the first quarter of 2007 (Ives, 2007, April 9). This slow growth turned to decline, and by the second half of 2010, the magazine's average newsstand sales had dropped 15.8 percent from 2009 (Kelly, 2011). Nevertheless, by leaning into the established gossip narratives that drove it to the top and the coverage of reality television celebrity that reliably filled pages by playing into those narratives, *Us* managed to stay afloat and even maintain its dominance in the celebrity weekly category during this time of crisis.

As I have illustrated in previous chapters, coverage of reality television cast members was a key component of the magazine's ability to rise and remain at the top of the genre, as these individuals offered a steady stream of content that fit neatly into the established narrative formulas of the magazine. In the early part of the decade, the increased attention to reality television celebrity in *Us Weekly* was closely aligned with the interests of its parent company, the Walt Disney Corporation. Centering much of the magazine's reality coverage on cast members from the *Bachelor/Bachelorette* franchise owned by Disney, Min and her staff helped transform these ordinary people into the celebrities we never knew we wanted, as a means to support the commercial aims of both the magazine and its larger parent company. This is not to suggest that cast members from other non-Disney programs were excluded from the magazine, as *Us Weekly* did tap into the overall popularity of the reality television genre through coverage of cast members from non-Disney programs like *Survivor* and *Joe Millionaire* throughout the decade. But it was the coverage of the *Bachelor/Bachelorette* franchise that both honed the cyclical celetoid mode of reality celebrity that helped *Us Weekly* begin to grow their own celebrity from a few franchise standouts, including Trista Rehn and Jenn Schefft. By offering a vehicle for the performance of the labor of ordinariness and celebrity lifestyle labor of reality television cast members, *Us Weekly* played an instrumental role in legitimating all forms of extraordinarily ordinary celebrity.

Min leaned heavily on coverage of reality television celebrities as the market began to shift, as a means to keep *Us Weekly* relevant and profitable. Of the sixty-one main *Us Weekly* cover stories dedicated to reality television celebrities between 2000 and 2009, over half of these covers (thirty-two) appeared between the time Wenner Media regained full ownership in August 2006 and December 2009, indicating the continued and intensified efforts by the magazine to cover reality television content and cast members. While this attention to reality television was, in part, tied to the genre's general popularity across media culture during the latter part of the decade, it was also an editorial strategy to attract readers in a time of increased competition by growing celebrities that fit the narrative formulas and cultural constructions of identity that already defined *Us Weekly*. For instance, given the success of the coverage of the *Bachelor/Bachelorette* franchise in the early part of the decade, these cyclical celetoids continued to be covered in earnest, appearing on an additional eight main cover stories and eight second-level cover stories between 2006 and 2009, and, as of this writing, routine coverage of the franchise continues in the magazine.[1] However, Min, always more interested in driving the narrative rather than simply responding to the cultural moment, began to expand the attempt to grow your own celebrity in the magazine to new, non-Disney reality cast members. Aiming to retain its young, female readership, *Us Weekly* increasingly inserted reality cast members into its established gossip formulas of body, beauty, fashion, and intimate relationships, effectively combining the labor of ordinariness with celebrity lifestyle labor to grow their own extraordinarily ordinary celebrities.

This chapter offers a close look at the one of the most covered and most enduring extraordinarily ordinary celebrities grown by *Us Weekly* during the early twenty-first century, Lauren Conrad. Lauren first entered the public eye as the star/narrator of the MTV docu-soap *Laguna Beach: The Real Orange County* (2004–2006), but it was during her time as the star/narrator of the successful spin-off, *The Hills* (2006–2010),[2] that *Us Weekly* became a key vehicle for moving Lauren from reality cast member to the pinnacle of extraordinarily ordinary celebrity. Throughout the latter part of the decade, Lauren was a frequent, almost ubiquitous presence in the magazine. She was a recurrent cover subject and regularly appeared across the photo and article features inside the magazine. In fact, between July 23, 2007, and December 15, 2008,[3] Lauren appeared in the magazine in some capacity on a nearly weekly basis, and her image was absent from only seven issues during this year-and-a-half time frame. Easily fitting into the magazine's already established gossip formulas and cultural constructions of identity, coverage of Lauren Conrad offered *Us Weekly* a steady stream of content that addressed its goal of appealing to a young, female readership by growing this ordinary girl into a celebrity. In short, Lauren was a girl just like us but a more stylized, idealized, and *celebritized* version of the feminine self to which readers could aspire. While she could have easily functioned as a celetoid, whose image quickly disappeared after her departure from the reality show that brought her into the public eye, a fate common to many of the reality celebrities covered by *Us Weekly*, the complex alchemy of the labor of ordinariness and celebrity lifestyle labor on which *Us Weekly* grew her extraordinarily ordinary celebrity continues to define her celebrity image today. No longer appearing on reality television, Lauren is now best known as a fashion designer, lifestyle blogger, and Instagram celebrity, and her image illustrates the ways in which the efforts to grow extraordinarily ordinary celebrity established in magazines like *Us Weekly* presaged the DIY celebrity of the contemporary social media age. Using the construction of Lauren's image in *Us Weekly* as a case study, this chapter will unpack the ways in which her extraordinarily ordinary image was grown in *Us Weekly* in the late 2000s and argue for the lasting impact of this form of celebrity on contemporary celebrity culture.

Covering *The Hills*

One major indicator of *Us Weekly*'s efforts at growing its own celebrity from the cast members of *The Hills* is the frequent and concentrated coverage of these reality cast members, particularly as cover stories. Though reality television cast members appeared throughout the magazine's pages during the 2000s, appearing on the cover suggests a higher level of fame because of the paramount importance of cover images to the magazine's newsstand sales, as discussed in chapter 2. Even though they did not begin to appear on covers until 2007, Lauren Conrad and the other cast members of *The Hills* were the second most frequent reality celebrity cover story subjects throughout the entire 2000–2009 time frame of this study, with only the cast members of the *Bachelor/Bachelorette* franchise appearing more often. However, even this second-place finish in total number of cover appearances belies the ubiquity of the *Hills* cast and the magazine's dedication to growing these cast members, particularly Lauren Conrad, into celebrities.

First, unlike the *Bachelor/Bachelorette* franchise's numerous appearances that were spread across the decade and, more importantly, across multiple seasons and cast members, the coverage of *The Hills* was more concentrated, with its cast members (primarily Lauren and her frenemy Heidi [Montag] Pratt) appearing in thirteen main cover stories and seventeen second-level cover stories between October 2007 and October 2009. In other words, the young women from *The Hills* appeared, in either primary or secondary-level stories, on nearly 30 percent of the covers of *Us Weekly* during this two-year time span. In contrast, one of the *Bachelor* franchise's most successful extraordinarily ordinary celebrities, Trista Sutter, accounted for only six of the franchise's twenty-two main story covers and six of the thirty-one second-level cover stories dedicated to the *Bachelor/Bachelorette* franchise. Trista's more frequent and enduring presence as an extraordinarily ordinary celebrity is not the common story of this franchise, as most cast members appeared on one or two covers and few *Bachelor* stars achieved lasting fame beyond the cyclical celetoid coverage discussed in chapter 2. Furthermore, despite an increased presence of reality television celebrities throughout the magazine, appearing on the cover remains evidence of the achievement of upper-level celebrity that few reality cast members achieved. *The Hills* cast members received the most covers of any other reality television program between October 2007 and December 2009. Other than the scandal-filled "summer of the Gosselins" discussed in chapter three when nine main cover stories (seven of them consecutive) were devoted to the stars of *Jon & Kate Plus 8*, only three other reality programs even appeared as a main cover story during the *Hills* reign: the already established cyclical celebrities of *The Bachelor/Bachelorette* with six main covers and *The Biggest Loser* and *The Real Housewives of New Jersey* with one main cover story each. The dominance of *Us Weekly* covers by the *Hills* cast represents a first example of the celebrification of these reality cast members, as appearing on the cover of a major celebrity weekly demonstrates one's celebrity value, particularly in terms of promoting the original program from which they emerged (see Klein, 2009, for a discussion of how extratextual coverage contributed to the success of *The Hills* as an MTV franchise). In other words, *Us Weekly*'s coverage helped establish the women of *The Hills* as more legitimate celebrities by inserting them into the established celebrity place of a celebrity weekly cover story.

Moreover, though the number of cover appearances indicates *Us Weekly*'s investment in growing these young women as *celebrities*, it does not fully represent the sheer ubiquity of *The Hills* cast members', particularly Lauren Conrad's, images within the pages of *Us Weekly* throughout the latter part of the decade as a means to reinforce that status through appeals to celebrity lifestyle labor. Most of the cover stories functioned as promotion narratives, framing *Us Weekly*'s "exclusive" access to "what you didn't see" on the show as a way to both keep readers invested in those show narratives and to offer Lauren a vehicle for the labor of ordinariness across intertextual spaces. But she was also a mainstay of lifestyle features, including Red Carpet, Hot Hollywood, and Loose Talk, which explicitly highlight the fashion, body, and lifestyle of celebrities. On July 28, 2008, she appeared in three different features, all of which speak to the ongoing preoccupation of *Us Weekly* with fashion, beauty, and body as a basis for celebrity. First, her jet-setting and glamorous lifestyle was on display in a Hot Pics photo of her alongside her costars Audrina Patridge and Lo Bosworth at "Intermix's VH1 Rock Honors party in L.A." the day before "hosting a Svedka fete at Lily Pond in East Hampton, NY" in the Hot Pics section (p. 30). Next, her fresh-faced youthful beauty was celebrated when she was paired with the actress Megan Fox in a photo feature titled "Age Face-Off" in which "100 people in NYC" were asked which star looked older, and 73 percent of respondents thought Fox "looked older," and implicitly less desirable, despite the fact Lauren "is almost four months older than the sultry Fox" (p. 32). Finally, as the center of a Star Style feature on "day-to-night dresses," a paparazzi photo of her in a maxidress placed at the center of the two-page feature offered inspiration for the dresses and accessories pictured in the article (How to: Day-to-night dresses, 2008, July 28, pp. 86–87, see fig. 5). Tellingly, not a single one of these examples included any reference to her status as a cast member of *The Hills*. Instead, it was simply assumed the reader would recognize Lauren Conrad as a celebrity whose youthful beauty and fashionable lifestyle make her worthy of coverage. This chapter will explore this interplay between the labor of ordinariness and celebrity lifestyle labor that shapes

Figure 5. Lauren in Star Style (July 28, 2008).

the coverage of Lauren's image within *Us Weekly* and how it was used to grow her into an extraordinarily ordinary celebrity.

"You Know What You Did!": Lauren and the Labor of Ordinariness

Us Weekly was certainly not the only extratextual media that covered *The Hills* cast members, as coverage of a celebrity's real and off-screen self across celebrity media is central to building the intertextuality necessary for celebrity status. Stories about Lauren regularly appeared in other gossip weeklies during her time on *The Hills*, as the drama stemming from the show's core story lines, such as Lauren's dating life, rumors she appeared in a sex tape,[4] and her ongoing feud with her former best friend Heidi Montag (Pratt), were covered across the celebrity gossip media as a means to promote the show and Lauren's celebrity. Her path to celebrity was also certainly aided by more legitimate extratextual media, as she was also a frequent cover girl on teen magazines (including *Seventeen*, *Cosmo Girl*, *Teen Vogue* [emphasizing the promotional use of her image, this was the magazine where she interned as part of the narrative of *The Hills*]) and in women's fashion magazines (including *Allure*, *Cosmo*, *Glamour*, and *Lucky*). But *Us Weekly* staked a claim as a primary purveyor of her off-screen self not simply through copious coverage of her but also by frequently framing that coverage as an "*Us* Exclusive." Promising the reader that here—and only here—would they get access to the real Lauren, *Us Weekly* showcased Lauren's labor of ordinariness to promote the show and, crucially, as a basis for growing her as a celebrity in *Us Weekly*. The *Us* exclusives promised readers the truth because their stories were centered on interviews with Lauren rather than relying on "sources close to the star" or other write-around techniques typically deployed by gossip magazines. Thus, *Us Weekly* positioned itself as a core text for the production of Lauren's celebrity image.

The growing of Lauren into a celebrity in *Us Weekly* through these *Us* exclusives (as well as its other coverage) points to the reciprocal yet contentious relationship that underscores the production of celebrity more generally. As Gamson (1994) argues, the "entertainment and media institutions are linked to each other: plainly put, producers need coverage and editors need subjects" (p. 66). *Us Weekly*'s young female readership paralleled the audience for *The Hills*, making it an ideal space for MTV to seek coverage of its reality cast members. Conversely, as a magazine facing an increasingly competitive celebrity media market, *Us Weekly* needed a way to set itself apart from other titles and online upstarts, and touting its exclusive access to celebrities, particularly those with whom a young female audience could identify, was one way it set itself apart from the pack. Of course, celebrities themselves need the editors as well, as magazines promote both a celebrity's current project and build the intertextual image that will (hopefully) endure beyond the end of a film or television program. Unlike A-list stars who rarely grant interviews to gossip media because of the subgenre's lack of legitimacy, reality television celebrities needed the exposure that *Us Weekly* can offer to both promote their shows and to build their intertextual images. Thus, MTV and Lauren were ready and willing to provide that exclusive access to *Us Weekly* to promote the show through Lauren's image. At the same time, *Us Weekly* would also look to grow celebrity in its own interest, moving away from more purely promotional narratives and deploying the celebrity image across a range of its own established gossip narratives. The *Us* exclusives about Lauren perform a balancing act between these interests: they tend to be rooted in promotion narratives that help promote the show itself but simultaneously use the attention to Lauren's labor of ordinariness to help shore up the appeals to authenticity that validate the magazine's parallel coverage of her celebrity lifestyle labor.

Overall, the majority of Lauren's cover appearances and related feature-length articles in *Us Weekly* work to extend the real Lauren seen on *The Hills*, offering audiences more exclusive or at least extended access to the young woman in the city narrative that is at the show's core. *The Hills* is steeped in "soap opera conventions to emotionally connect the viewer with Lauren's 'real life' melodrama," particularly her struggles at work, efforts to navigate her female friendships, and attempts to find love in the city (Leppert & Wilson, 2008, para. 16). For instance, an *Us* exclusive second-level cover story titled

"Secrets of *The Hills*" offered an interview with Lauren in which she "discusses all the juicy stuff you didn't see this season [two]" (Bruce, 2007, p. 78). This is a clear promotion narrative in which Lauren dishes exclusively with *Us* about the latest drama on *The Hills* as a means to keep readers interested as the show went on hiatus at the end of season 2. (The season finale aired on April 2, 2007, a few days before the magazine's on-sale date of April 6, 2007.) In the accompanying article, Lauren offers behind-the-scenes insight into major plot points from the just-wrapped season, including details on the big finale reveal that her former best friend Heidi Montag moved out of their shared apartment as a result of the ongoing feud about Heidi's relationship with her then-boyfriend Spencer Pratt and "new BFF Audrina" Patridge moved in (ibid.). This promotion narrative is a performance of the labor of ordinariness because Lauren is not a television writer detailing a fictional narrative but the person who lived these experiences revealing the emotional truths of her real life. Her emotions are, indeed, at the forefront of her interview. For instance, in discussing her former fling Brody Jenner's hookup with Lauren's friend Jen Bunney, a major plot point of the season that was allegedly orchestrated by Heidi and Spencer, Lauren reveals the hurt that she "didn't know" that Heidi was involved until she saw it on television. She says, "[Heidi] said 'It was all Jen,' and I believed her. Everything we're doing is recorded by cameras, so we get caught. I was so angry after I watched that episode. I was shaking" (ibid.). Lauren's real life is depicted on the show, but the *Us* exclusive interview deepens the readers' access to the emotional impact of that narrative in ways that help promote the show while simultaneously shoring up Lauren's authenticity as a girl dealing with real-life intimate relationships.

Similarly, in the run-up to the premiere of season 3, Lauren appeared in another *Us* exclusive on August 13, 2007, where she entices readers with details of "what will surely be the show's most talked-about moments—and what you won't see on TV" (Guarente, 2007, August 13, p. 70). She gives readers her view on the sex tape rumors—also depicted on the show as the work of the series villains, Heidi and Spencer—that emerged that summer in the gossip media (including *Us Weekly*) and would become a major plot point in the upcoming season. Though this is promotional work tying Lauren to the narrative of the upcoming season, the interview also reinforces her ordinariness by showcasing the emotional impact of these rumors as a way for readers to relate to her. She says, "When a friend stabs you in the back, it's almost bittersweet, because you know you've lost a friend. But in a way, it makes you appreciate all the people in your life who are good. I have all these amazing friends who would never do that to me" (pp. 70–71). Lauren's role as the good girl with whom the audience would want to be friends calls up her image on the show but also is central to *Us Weekly*'s effort to extend that image outside of the show's narrative. *Us Weekly*'s celebrification of Lauren relies on the maintenance of her underlying authenticity as a girl who is just like us. Throughout the run of the series, *Us* would be a place where the drama of the show played out in greater detail, allowing the readers more access to the real story (from both Lauren's and Heidi's perspectives) and simultaneously using that realness and authenticity as a basis from which to grow Lauren into a celebrity.

While *Us Weekly* too relies on this ordinariness as part of its coverage of Lauren Conrad and the other cast members of *The Hills*, it is used as the building block for Lauren's extraordinary celebrity self. This upholds the core myth of stardom that those who are special will rise to the top and live the glamorous celebrity lifestyle but will continue to deserve fame by virtue of the real and authentic self that remains at the core of the image. In contemporary celebrity, specialness is not tied to talent or skill but rather to the labor of ordinariness or the successful presentation of the authentic self within the public sphere. Thus, Lauren is not simply just like us; she is the ideal version of the appropriate feminine self at the turn of the twenty-first century and is therefore worthy of celebrity. Embodying the sensibilities of postfeminism as discussed by Angela McRobbie (2004) and Rosalind Gill (2007), Lauren's persona on the show and in the pages of *Us Weekly* relies on a "grammar of individualism" in which her choices to cultivate an appropriate feminine self—one marked by both her creative labor in the fashion industry and her lifestyle labor in her conspicuous consumption and seemingly effortless successes to maintain her "style" and "beauty"—are marked as authentic choices rather than choices made within the contexts of a consumerist patriarchy (Gill, 2007, p. 153). Framing Lauren as "an ordinary girl in the context of an extraordinary 'real' life," *Us Weekly* grows her into an extraordinarily ordinary celebrity by validating those choices as deserving of fame (Leppert & Wilson, 2008, para. 15).

"Star Style": Lauren and Celebrity Lifestyle Labor

Alice Leppert and Julie Wilson (2008) point out that on the show "Lauren's extraordinary status is paradoxically produced by a representational insistence on her ordinariness, that is, by refusing to allude to Lauren's actual reality stardom within the discourse of *The Hills*" (para. 12; see also Affuso, 2009). The show produces her image as one that is at once eminently relatable because she lives out the life concerns germane to young women at this cultural moment yet set against "the backdrop of trendy clubs, alluring work settings, and stylized apartments" and begins to elevate her ordinariness to extraordinariness but explicitly stops short of showing her as a celebrity (para. 15). For instance, despite their routine appearance at the sorts of celebrity-studded red carpet events that are a mainstay of *Us Weekly* coverage of celebrity culture and their promotional labor on behalf of other media, fashion, and beauty products, the narrative of *The Hills* explicitly excludes this part of their real lives from the show. The executive producer Liz Gately promises the show offers "the access that [audiences aren't] getting in the tabloids. They're getting their private life" (qtd. in Stack, 2008, p. 26). The *Entertainment Weekly* writer Tim Stack (2008) notes that red carpet events at which the young cast members routinely appear are intentionally not filmed by the producers and that the *Hills* production crews also must work to shoot around the paparazzi that follow the cast members around to ensure the ordinary and private-life narrative of the program is maintained.

Whereas MTV diligently worked to keep Lauren's celebrity out of *The Hills*, *Us Weekly* reapplies it like a fresh coat of lipstick, glamorizing Lauren's ordinariness as a means to grow her from a reality television cast member into an extraordinarily ordinary celebrity. Attention to her celebrity lifestyle labor was included in some form in nearly all of their stories about her, and in some, it provided the sole reason for her coverage. Her ordinariness was often presented as the key to her entrance into and staying power within celebrity culture, using it as a justification for the continued attention to and social value of her image. Moving away from the promotional narratives centered on the sex tape scandal, her first solo main cover story on November 12, 2007, instead offered readers a glimpse of her real Hollywood dating life and advice on looking for love, highlighting Lauren as a relatable girl who just happens to be a celebrity. Though she dishes about "dating in Hollywood" and how "fame has changed [her] dating life," her experiences are ultimately relatable to the average reader (Appel, Baker, & Vituscka, 2007, November 12, pp. 59–61). She breezily discusses staying friends with ex-boyfriends and pursuing "friends with benefits" relationships and shares some of her worst first-date experiences in a question-and-answer interview format that makes the reader feel they are having a chat with a girlfriend (ibid.). This relatability is further intensified through the continued reinforcement of the norms of femininity that already shape the magazine. Lauren is attractive but doesn't try too hard: "Normally I wear my makeup the same on a date as I do in the daytime; it's important to be yourself" (p. 63). She endures bad dates on her quest to find Mr. Right: "I've gone out with guys like that—who were rude to the waiter or put people down—and, literally right after dinner, I acted sick so I could go home" (p. 62). She worries about her appearance: "I almost always wear a dress on the first date, and get a second opinion on the outfit from a friend" (p. 63). She has celebrity crushes: "I have always loved Mark Wahlberg. He's just so cute!" (p. 61). In short, she is performing the right kind of youthful feminine ordinariness that the magazine already values and to which its readers are meant to aspire.

Additionally, through its attention to Lauren at red carpet events, in style features, and staged fashion features that have little to no tie back to narratives on *The Hills* (and, as previously mentioned, were intentionally ignored as part of Lauren's real life on the show), *Us Weekly* also made her celebrity lifestyle labor the primary focus of their coverage of her. This attention to Lauren's celebrity lifestyle labor serves, ultimately, as a means to commodify her celebrity image, branding her ordinary and authentic lifestyle and selling it back to consumers through a range of products. Leppert and Wilson (2008) suggest this is particularly salient to Lauren's image, arguing, "MTV provides the viewer who aspires to be Lauren or be like Lauren with never ending opportunities to consume as Lauren does . . . [through] articulation of Lauren's star image to a feminine fashion and consumer culture" (para. 2). They usefully unpack the ways in which MTV promotes Lauren's celebrity brand implicitly through the narratives and aesthetics of *The Hills* and more explicitly by pushing products related to the show on MTV.com and "Living the *Hill$* Life" rebroadcasts of episodes "with running pop-up commentary detailing the costs of clothes, accessories, and cars of *Hills* cast members" (para. 26). This sort of explicit lifestyle branding and celebrity commodification is precisely the purview of the celebrity weeklies, and Lauren's image fit neatly into the magazine's established discourses of consumerism and femininity. Relying on Lauren's ordinariness but, as an extratextual source, not beholden to a need to hide her celebrity to maintain it, *Us Weekly*'s coverage of Lauren's celebrity lifestyle labor is thus essential to the production of her as an extraordinarily ordinary celebrity.

Lauren was a regular fixture of fashion-oriented photo features, appearing, for instance, six times between September 2007 and November 2008 in the Red Carpet fashion photo feature, a prime space of celebrity lifestyle labor discussed in chapter 3. Red Carpet is not a feature that mocks celebrity fashion choices or seeks to catch celebrities "off guard, unkempt, and unready" to expose the mask of glamour (Holmes, 2005). Instead, it frames the celebrity as naturally fashionable and chic in all moments of her life, tying her celebrity value to her ability to properly perform a consumerist femininity. In addition to appearing in this feature alongside traditional celebrities, including the actresses Gwyenth Paltrow and Ali Larter on May 19, 2008, and the actress Renée Zellweger and actress / pop star Jennifer Lopez on September 29, 2008, Lauren had an entire Red Carpet devoted to only her "chic fall fashion" on November 17, 2008. As with other Red Carpet photo spreads that document the work of being a celebrity across various celebrity places, the photos in this solo feature are paparazzi photos taken either at celebrity events, such as Lauren arriving for her appearance on *The Late Show with David Letterman*, attending Fashion Week events (including her own fashion show), or snapped on the street as the celebrity goes about her glamorous life in glamorous clothing. Lauren also appeared in the signature *Us Weekly* photo feature Who Wore It Best? eleven times between June 2007 and August 2009 and won every pairing except one (where she narrowly missed the top spot and came in second of three). Here, she is not only successfully performing celebrity lifestyle labor through her fashion choices; she is *more* successful than the other celebrities paired against her, solidifying her role in the magazine as an aspirational yet attainable style icon.

Such coverage of her as a fashion icon worked in tandem with the image constructed on *The Hills*, since the show tracked her efforts to start a career in fashion—she began the series attending the Fashion Institute of Design and Merchandising in Los Angeles and later interned at *Teen Vogue*. However, as a media space for the performance of celebrity lifestyle labor, *Us Weekly* had the ability to go further in terms of inserting her into the fashion world by virtue of her celebrity status. A February 26, 2007, *Us* Exclusive gave readers a peek at "Lauren Conrad's Fashion Diary," detailing the "fashion fanatic['s] trip to New York City's glamorous Mercedes-Benz Fashion Week" (Lauren Conrad's fashion diary, 2007, February 26, p. 78). While a fashion magazine intern *may* be able to attend these events as part of their job, Lauren's trip, which was not featured in any way on the show, was a glamorous experience that is likely not typical of most interns. *Us Weekly* tagged along throughout Lauren's week in New York City, documenting her extraordinary experience through photos of her visit to the design house Luca Luca to pick out a dress to wear to their runway show, sitting front row at various designers' runway shows (alongside other celebrities like the pop star JC Chasez and the MTV VJ Vanessa Minnillo), and receiving "cute watches" in a gift bag at the designer Betsey Johnson's show (p. 78–79). Yet even these explicit moments of celebrity lifestyle labor are counterbalanced with appeals to her ordinariness. For instance, in the accompanying interview, Lauren discusses being star struck when she "spot[s] [the musician] Lenny Kravitz and [the actress] Michelle Rodriguez" at runway shows and being surprised by "pals" with a birthday cake and balloons, albeit at the hot New York City nightclub Marquee, reinforcing her as a normal girl who just happens to get access to these celebrity events and experiences (ibid.). She lives an extraordinary lifestyle but, at the core, is ordinary and just like us.

Us Weekly also offered readers a glimpse of some of Lauren's creative labor as a designer through coverage of her eponymous fashion line and other design efforts. To maintain her ordinariness, this work was explicitly left out of the narrative of *The Hills*, even though Lauren was a fashion and design student, and, as Leppert and Wilson (2008) point out, MTV was a financial partner in her first clothing line, the Lauren Conrad Collection (para. 4). *Us Weekly*, in contrast, can easily assimilate the creative labor of fashion design into the larger celebrity lifestyle coverage of Lauren through their appeals to her as a style icon. For instance, when Lauren was tapped, alongside the *Project Runway 4* winner Christian Siriano, to be "the first celebrity designers to create gowns for [the Emmy Awards'] 'trophy girls,' the two women who hand over statuettes and guide beaming winners off the stage," *Us Weekly* celebrated her achievement in a two-page *Us* Exclusive article and photo spread showcasing Lauren's design process and inspirations (Meneses, 2008, p. 78). Bestowing on Lauren the accolade of "*Us* celeb designer of the year," the article reminds readers that her "luxe-meets-casual clothes" are available "at more than 500 boutiques" and at "shoplaurenconrad.com" while also offering a sneak peek at the "simple silhouette" she designed for the awards show by updating "a design from a past collection" (p. 79). Lauren's celebrity is in part reinforced by her creative labor as a fashion designer, not as a reality television cast member, but the article primarily serves as a reminder to readers of how they can achieve Lauren's glamorous style through the purchase of items from her clothing line.

While Lauren's tie to labor in the fashion industry remained relevant to the coverage of her in *Us Weekly*, it was typically subsumed by a more general appeal to her as a style icon. In other words, Lauren is not a style icon because she works in the fashion industry; she works in the fashion industry because she already embodies the idealized feminine body and style. This is most evident in *Us Weekly*'s repeated use of Lauren in its various Hot Hollywood style awards and annual "Style Issue" features—*Us Weekly* franchise exclusives—alongside more traditional celebrities. Just after the first season of *The Hills* ended in August 2006, Lauren was the only reality television cast member named as one of the fifteen Hot Hollywood "Fresh Faces of 2006" (Fresh faces of 2006, 2006, October 2). A large page-and-a-half photo of Lauren opened the article, which, like a cover photo, suggests her celebrity has enough value to draw audiences to the content. Even in this moment of extraordinariness, exemplified by the glamorous photo and the accompanying text reminding readers that "MTV renewed her hit show," readers are also reminded of the authenticity at the core of her image (p. 80). She dishes about her newly single status, having split with boyfriend Jason Wahler on the previous season of *The Hills*, saying, "I forgot how fun it is to be single. I even went out and bought a 'single' wardrobe!" (ibid.). Even in this moment of ordinariness, discourses of fashion and consumption shape her image.

This Hot Hollywood appearance was the first of many "official" recognitions of her as a style icon in the magazine. The following May, she was named one of the Hot Hollywood "Style Winners: 7 in '07 . . . honor[ing] the 14 men and women suddenly at the peak of chic thanks to their unique elegance" (Bartolomeo, Mehalic, & Reinstein, 2007, May 7). She was also a Hot Hollywood "Power Player of 2007" and was named the Hot Hollywood Style "Celebrity Designer of the Year" in 2008 (Agresti et al., 2007, October 1; Agresti, 2008, April 28). Lauren was twice included on the cover of *Us Weekly*'s annual fall "Style Issue," alongside her *Hills* costars Audrina and Whitney on October 15, 2007, and, in a move distancing her from her reality television origins, alongside the pop star Taylor Swift and the pop star / actress Hilary Duff on October 13, 2008 (see fig. 6).

These cover stories feature a "fashion roundtable" discussion with the stars about their favorite fall fashions, giving the reader insight into real fashion and style tips from these glamorous and extraordinary celebrities. That is, they may

Figure 6. Lauren in the 2008 annual "Style Issue" (October 13, 2008).

be putting together looks for the red carpet or worrying about what they are wearing when they are snapped by paparazzi, but they also share the same sorts of fashion and body concerns as the average reader. The October 13, 2008, roundtable includes Lauren discussing "always trying to hide my thighs, whether it's with a longer t-shirt or a skirt with a natural waist" and revealing that she is "really lazy" about going to get her hair colored (Bromley, 2008, October 13, p. 76). Through such appeals to Lauren's authentic self, this celebrity lifestyle labor is at once glamorous and accessible.

Lauren's celebrity lifestyle labor is at its most commodified in her frequent appearances in regular style-oriented features that more explicitly connect celebrity to consumer products, such as the almost catalog-like feature Star Style, which showcases celebrity fashion and makeup alongside how to buy them. In a previously mentioned Star Style from July 28, 2008, titled "How To: Day-to-Night Dresses," Lauren is featured in the center of a two-page photo spread telling readers how to appropriately style minidresses and maxidresses to move from day to night (How to: Day-to-night dresses, 2008, July 28, see fig. 5). She is, notably, the only celebrity whose photograph appears in this feature, and the caption details her outfit by reinforcing the high-end glamour of her celebrity lifestyle, saying, "LAUREN CONRAD glammed up a maxidress from her own label with Valentino's $2,150 gold Nauge bag" (pp. 86–87). Here, Lauren's maxidress, like Lauren herself, is framed as ordinary but able to be "glammed up" and made extraordinary by the designer bag. The tie to consumption is reinforced as Lauren is surrounded by more dresses, accessories, and shoes that help instruct the reader how to get a similar look, including prices and where to buy these items. Catalog-style features like Star Style appear throughout the magazine, masquerading as content rather than just ads by adding some level of celebrity content. But the tie to celebrity is paramount, as it is the successful articulation of the celebrity image and the attributes of identity she embodies to the product that makes a strong branding connection. Elizabeth Currid-Halkett (2010) says, "We buy products if they are plausible extensions of the stars" (p. 183–184). Similarly, the regular catalog-style feature Us Buzzzz-o-Meter also appears in every issue and lists the "people, places, and things that are keeping *Us* abuzz," connecting readers to the celebrity lifestyle through products, frequently picturing the product and only listing the celebrity's name, such as Lauren's February 18, 2008, listing as a celebrity who "loves" Aerie Lingerie (*Us* buzzzz-o-meter, 2008, February 18). The reader does not even need to see Lauren wearing the product; rather, just the connection of her name to it is enough to reinforce its desirability. Lauren's image is deployed here because it is fashionable and extraordinary, something to which readers should aspire. But it is attainable because she is ordinary and just like us. In short, she is an ideal extraordinarily ordinary celebrity.

Growing the Fame-Damaged Celebrity

As the construction of Lauren's image in *Us Weekly* illustrates, the extraordinarily ordinary celebrity is a celebrity grown to fit the established gossip narratives of the magazine to benefit both the magazine and the cast member (and the show from which she originated). Lauren, as with other extraordinarily ordinary celebrities like Trista (Rehn) Sutter, embodies the normative ideologies of femininity to which the young female readership of *Us Weekly* are meant to aspire. Coverage of her ongoing struggles as she looks for love, navigates close friendships, and pursues her career dreams reminds readers that she is just like us. Parallel coverage of a glamorous and consumption-based lifestyle outside of the show builds on this ordinariness, suggesting first that Lauren deserves this lifestyle because she remains true to her real and authentic self and subsequently that being like Lauren can be achieved through the proper consumption of fashion and beauty commodities. In short, it is not simply increased coverage of a reality cast member that constructs extraordinarily ordinary celebrity but the *right kind* of coverage of the *right kind* of self. Thus, not every reality cast member who is covered in the magazine performing the labor of ordinariness and celebrity lifestyle labor will acquire extraordinarily ordinary celebrity.

Indeed, the *Hills* villainess Heidi Montag (Pratt) was featured on the cover of *Us Weekly* more times than Lauren, with five of the thirteen covers including cast members of *The Hills* featuring Heidi alone compared to just two featuring a solo Lauren and one featuring the two together.[5] Tellingly, unlike Lauren's two annual "Style Issue" covers, Heidi never appeared on a style-oriented cover nor on any cover that placed her alongside traditional celebrities. But her multiple covers and overall frequent appearances in the magazine indicates the important corollary of the rise of the extraordinarily ordinary celebrity—the fame-damaged celebrity. As discussed in chapter 3, narratives of fame damage are intrinsic to celebrity culture, particularly in judging the authenticity of an individual who has acquired the wealth and glamour associated with celebrity status. To maintain the myth of meritocracy that underscores the hierarchy of celebrity culture, the individual who is offered access to the spoils of celebrity lifestyles must be read as *deserving* such access through the performance of the right kind of labor of ordinariness. The inability to be properly ordinary beneath the extraordinariness of celebrity may preclude the reality cast member from acquiring lasting extraordinarily ordinary status, as with the example of Evan Marriott in chapter 3, but it does not necessarily stop *Us Weekly* from covering that individual and profiting from such coverage. As a media source rooted in gossip, scandal and moral failures are important to *Us Weekly*'s narrative formulas and its economic bottom line. Already established as the villainess foil to Lauren's good girl heroine on *The Hills*, the coverage of Heidi as a fame-damaged celebrity ultimately serves to reinforce Lauren's authentic, deserved, and extraordinarily ordinary fame. Furthermore, this continued coverage of Heidi's failures is a means for the magazine to sell issues, as well as normative ideologies about how a female star should act. Thus, in addition to benefitting from the construction of extraordinarily ordinary celebrities like Lauren, *Us Weekly* had an economic and social interest in also covering those fame whores who act as cautionary tales.

Heidi vs. Lauren: Reinforcing Extraordinariness through Fame Damage

Leppert and Wilson (2008) argue that, via both Lauren's voiceover narration of the series and the reliance on soap opera conventions, *The Hills* places Lauren in the center of the show's narrative. They argue, "Most *Hills* episodes revolve around one personal problem or set of related problems that Lauren discusses with several of her friends. As in soap operas, conversation is the crux of *The Hills*, but here conversation most always revolves to varying degrees *around Lauren* in the service of elaborating her point of view. . . . When Lauren is not discussing she is being discussed" (para. 17, emphasis mine). As the villainess to Lauren's good girl in the narrative of *The Hills*, Heidi (and her boyfriend Spencer) was always positioned outside of—and as a threat to—Lauren's role at the center of the narrative. *Us Weekly*'s promotional narratives around the show reinforced this villain status, framing Heidi as a bad friend for ultimately choosing Spencer over her friendship with Lauren, such as in the *Us* Exclusive "My Side of the Story" from August 13, 2007, in which Lauren laments the loss of the friendship, saying, "At this point, Heidi has just done too much to me that I don't need a friend like that" (Guarente, 2007, August 13, p. 68). In the May 19, 2008, cover story "The Plot to Destroy Lauren," Heidi and Spencer are accused of maliciously conspiring to enact "Operation Attack Lauren" through their "open discussion and proliferation of stories regarding the rumored—but never proven—sex tape involving Conrad and her ex—Jason Wahler" both on the show and in the gossip press (Agresti, 2008, May 19, p. 59). These promotional narratives keep Heidi in the public eye but only in relation to Lauren and ultimately serve to reinforce Lauren as the real celebrity who deserves her fame and Heidi as a desperate wannabe spitefully trying to push her out of the way.

When Heidi is the subject of the cover story or interview, the stories are primarily promotional narratives that draw the reader back to the relationship dramas depicted on the show in ways that often explicitly bring Lauren back to the center of the story. Though the majority of these cover stories foreground Heidi's point of view, in a mirroring of the narrative structure of *The Hills*, they always specifically discuss Lauren and also frequently include sidebar articles about Lauren's life. For instance, in the March 17, 2008, *Us* Exclusive main cover story interview that centered on the cheating allegations that led Heidi to move out of her shared apartment with Spencer during the season 4 finale of *The Hills*, she is asked, "Did you ever think Lauren Conrad was right?" and "Who's more successful at love: you or she?" (Reinstein, 2008, March 17, p. 56). Even the December 8, 2008, cover story about Heidi and Spencer's elopement included a discussion of whether Heidi and Spencer thought "Lauren Conrad will be happy" for them (O'Leary, 2008, December 8, p. 52). Furthermore, key to their villainous narrative was the ways in which Heidi and Spencer were largely read as "trying too hard" to become famous outside of the show, falsifying any sense of realness in order to gain greater notoriety. The aforementioned cover stories in which Heidi discusses personal details of her relationship with Spencer, including a breakup, cheating rumors, and a reconciliation, are more sympathetic and do highlight an ordinary girl struggling with her romantic relationship—a topic to which many readers could relate as they do to Lauren's romantic ups and downs. However, subsequent coverage undercuts the sincerity of these pieces, suggesting that even the couple's breakup and elopement was done for the benefit of the media attention. In August 2007, Lauren's pal Audrina confided to *Us Weekly* that "Heidi and Spencer . . . want attention and they'll use Lauren's name to get it," and in May 2008, a "source close to Conrad" told *Us Weekly*, "The only reason Spencer and Heidi are [talking about the sex tape] is to make themselves relevant again" (Guarente, 2007, August 13, p. 70; Agresti, 2008, May 19, p. 60). These stories certainly are promotional, as these are events that relate to the upcoming season's narratives, but they notably reinforce the show's focus *on Lauren* in the magazine's coverage of Heidi. Moreover, whereas Lauren's first solo cover story, "New Dating Rules," and her subsequent "Style Issue" covers work to distance her from the show's narrative through appeals to celebrity lifestyle labor—and notably do not feature any questions or content about Heidi—Heidi's covers keep her firmly tied to the narrative of the show itself and to her relationship to Lauren.

Heidi is shown engaged in various attempts at celebrity lifestyle labor, but such efforts are typically framed as fame damage and further proof of her inauthenticity. Stories about her off-screen life are typically viewed skeptically, suggesting to readers that she is simply seeking attention and working to build her celebrity.[6] A Hot Stuff piece about her (first) engagement to Spencer includes discussion of the "3.5-carat lemon lavender amethyst ring set in 18-karat white gold" and a photo of Heidi wearing the ring in public, but the article concludes with a statement that "at least one source tells *Us* all this is likely a public-relations prank" intended to promote the couple and draw audiences back to the show (Hot stuff: Heidi & Spencer engaged! 2007, June 11, p. 58). Just as the good-girl persona cultivated around Lauren in the show extended into the magazine's coverage of her and provides the foundation for her subsequent extraordinarily ordinary status, the specters of villainy and fakery haunt even the most earnest attempts to grow Heidi's celebrity. Back-to-back covers in December 2008 covering first her elopement with Spencer and then "her mom's fury" at the marriage first offer a typical moment of celebrity lifestyle labor in which Heidi offers all the details on the dress, flowers, and ceremony, alongside exclusive photos of the event, to paint a picture of a happy couple and their glamorous, if impromptu, wedding that is then undercut by her mother's claims of Spencer's manipulation and control over Heidi, echoing a larger narrative from *The Hills* about the ongoing tension between Spencer and Heidi's family that mirrors the feud with Lauren and suggests all of Heidi's relationships suffer because of her allegiance to Spencer (O'Leary, 2008, December 8; Agresti, 2008, December 15). Heidi's appearances in *Us Weekly* are certainly tied to her willingness to be photographed and interviewed and the magazine's ongoing need for content, but her inability to acquire the same sort of extraordinarily ordinary fame as Lauren reinforces the importance of authenticity and ordinariness as the core to the truly extraordinarily ordinary celebrity.

Conclusion: Lauren after *The Hills*

Most reality cast members find themselves unable to transfer their images outside of reality television, as their particular image remains tied to the character/brand established within the show's narrative. In his discussion of reality competition programs, Hunter Hargraves (2018) argues that, with few exceptions, "the best most former contestants of reality programmes can hope for is to be invited back to serve as a mentor or a judge on future seasons or a contestant in an all-star season" (p. 6). Many docu-soap cast members are similarly constrained to either joining celebrity versions of reality programs—such as Heidi and Spencer's stint on the U.S. version of *I'm A Celebrity . . . Get Me Out of Here!* (2009), the British version of *Celebrity Big Brother* (2013), and *Marriage Boot Camp: Reality Stars* (2015) or the appearance of multiple former *Bachelor/Bachelorette* cast members on ABC's *Dancing with the Stars*—or finding new life on spin-offs of the original series, such as Whitney Port's move to *The City* (2008–2010) after departing *The Hills* in 2008. This extends these individuals' time in the public eye and indeed often also in the pages of *Us Weekly*, but most are unable to move their celebrity beyond the confines of reality television.

Since departing from *The Hills* in 2009, Lauren has not appeared on any other reality television programming yet continues to enjoy an extraordinarily ordinary celebrity status. She is unique in this regard among the extraordinarily ordinary celebrities emerging in *Us Weekly* during the early 2000s. The decade's other most covered extraordinarily ordinary reality celebrity, Trista (Rehn) Sutter, followed up her stints on *The Bachelor* and *The Bachelorette* (and, of course, her televised wedding special) with appearances on ABC's *Dancing with the Stars* (2005) and *Marriage Boot Camp: Reality Stars* (2014). I argue the construction of Lauren as an extraordinarily ordinary celebrity within *Us Weekly* enabled her to avoid the reality fame cycle that traps the image within reality television by connecting her ordinary and authentic self to a deserved and idealized celebrity lifestyle and then branding that lifestyle and making it seem accessible to the audience and allowing her to build and maintain a high level of extraordinarily ordinary celebrity.

Lauren has successfully parlayed the style icon image central to her *Us Weekly* persona into a lasting form of extraordinarily ordinary celebrity. She has launched two more clothing lines (a high-end line called Paper Crown and, in partnership with U.S. mass retailer Kohl's, a more affordable line, LC Lauren Conrad) and written nine best-selling books, including both fiction titles and style and beauty guides; she maintains a successful lifestyle blog (laurenconrad.com) and related Instagram account (@laurenconrad) and in 2013 launched The Little Market, a nonprofit online fair-trade home decor and accessories outlet selling products that are "beautifully handmade by thousands of individual artisans located around the world" (TheLittleMarket, 2017). As a celebrity lifestyle blogger, Lauren embodies the same normative ideologies that shaped her extraordinarily ordinary image in *Us Weekly*: she is just like us in her values and pursuits (home, family, career success), while also living an aspirational and stylized lifestyle that is commodified and sold back to the reader. As with Trista Sutter's continued appearance in *Us Weekly* as she cycled through the appropriate work of being a woman in her post-*Bachelor* life—marriage, baby, losing the baby weight—Lauren's lasting extraordinarily ordinary celebrity is rooted in her successful performance of changing norms of feminine behavior as she ages. She has moved beyond the entry-level work in the fashion industry to the position of a "girl boss" who built her own fashion and lifestyle companies, a deeply gendered mode of self-branding in which "women must perform as self-entrepreneurial, self-promotional workers on equal footing with their male colleagues yet still be invested in and appear willing to perform traditional gender roles" (Wilson, 2010, p. 34). Intimate relationships remain central to her image, but she has shifted from feuding with her frenemy Heidi and dealing with boy drama to finding a husband and having a baby, all while building a lifestyle brand that presents her as a "millennial Martha Stewart" (Berger, 2016, p. 118). This plays out in her continued appearances in *Us Weekly*, as she was again tapped for the cover of the annual "Fall Fashion" issue in September 2013 and in an *Us* Exclusive main cover story about her "dream wedding" in 2014. Moreover, she appeared as the magazine's "guest entertainment editor" in 2016 and 2017, penning multiple columns offering readers guidance on throwing successful and stylish parties at home, melding her professional and personal selves into a single extraordinarily ordinary image.

The most important change to Lauren's celebrity in its contemporary incarnation is the ways in which social media enables her and other extraordinarily ordinary celebrities like her to refine and control her authentic persona outside of the control of *Us Weekly* and to speak more directly to her audience. However, the interplay between glamorous and quotidian, between stylized and authentic, and between just being yourself and doing the work of living a celebrity lifestyle that echoes across her image is directly related to the same discourses that grew her into an extraordinarily ordinary celebrity in *Us Weekly* in the early

2000s. The ability of her image to transition in this way speaks to the ongoing relevance of the work of just being yourself that shaped *Us Weekly*'s coverage of reality television celebrities to the broader shift in celebrity culture toward ordinariness. The final chapter of this book contemplates the lessons learned from *Us Weekly*'s role in the construction and circulation of the extraordinarily ordinary celebrity and the magazine's continued place within celebrity culture.

CONCLUSION

THE FUTURE OF THE EXTRAORDINARILY ORDINARY CELEBRITY

As the twenty-first century entered its second decade, *Us Weekly* helped redefine contemporary celebrity culture and the role of extratextual media within that culture in multiple ways. The magazine's formulaic style—defined by photo-heavy articles, a cheeky yet loving tone, and reliance on gossip narratives that simultaneously reveled in the glamour of celebrity lifestyles and revealed how stars were ultimately just like us—propelled it to the top of the celebrity weekly market and was widely imitated across the genre. As competition between gossip media outlets increased, *Us Weekly*'s turn toward coverage of reality television cast members—both as celetoids and as more lasting extraordinarily ordinary celebrities—was instrumental to maintaining both its cultural impact and economic success. Beginning in the early 2000s, *Us Weekly* increasingly relied on reality cast members to fill its pages and to distinguish itself from the competition through exclusive access to the very reality celebrities it helped to cultivate. This coverage grew slowly, with just a few covers in the early 2000s devoted to reality television that primarily focused on promotion narratives explicitly tied to the shows themselves. But by 2009, reality television coverage accounted for 30 percent of all covers for the year, as *Us Weekly* increasingly combined these promotion narratives with attention to the cast members' lives outside of the show. Such coverage was a natural extension of *Us Weekly*'s existing focus on the private and ordinary self as the core of the celebrity image, shoring up the magazine's already successful gossip formulas through attention to a new crop of celebrity personas who neatly embodied the underlying white, heteronormative, hyperfeminine, and consumerist narratives that shaped *Us Weekly*'s view of celebrity culture.

Though multiple industrial forces were involved in this shift in celebrity culture, *Us Weekly*'s role as vehicle for the rise of the extraordinarily ordinary celebrity points to the continued centrality of extratextual media to the construction and circulation of celebrity images. Through the private-focused stories and scandals the magazine helped to create, reality celebrities were taken out of the narrative boundaries of their reality television programs and given the necessary intertextuality to build and maintain a more durable celebrity. *Us Weekly*'s continual coverage of reality television cast members helped legitimize just being yourself as a path to fame while simultaneously delineating the right kind of self that must be performed to escape into the more rarified realm of celebrity. Furthermore, by inserting reality cast members as ordinary individuals into the glitz and glamour of celebrity lifestyles, *Us Weekly* reinforced the consumerist spectacle that lies at the heart of celebrity culture itself as a mode of celebrity production. The extraordinarily ordinary celebrity is not simply about just being yourself but being the right kind of self—a self that reaffirms the hyperfeminine, consumerist vision of womanhood espoused by *Us Weekly*. Thus, the efforts to grow reality cast members, such as Trista Sutter and Lauren Conrad, into extraordinarily ordinary celebrities through appeals to the labor of ordinariness and celebrity lifestyle labor are significant symptoms of the larger shift toward ordinariness within celebrity culture

The Continued Role of Extraordinarily Ordinary Celebrity in *Us Weekly*

While coverage of traditional celebrities certainly continued as the twenty-first century progressed, *Us Weekly*'s attention to various forms of reality television celebrity exploded in the 2010s, a clear indication of both the economic and social success of this new category of celebrity. The first five years of the decade (2010–2014) saw a massive growth in cover stories—a central way the magazine sells itself to consumers—dedicated to reality television celebrities. My analysis of *Us Weekly* covers from 2010 through 2014 revealed that reality cast members were featured in 121 main cover stories (or 47 percent of the main covers during these five years) and in 230 second-level cover stories, compared to 61 main cover stories and 85 second-level cover stories across the entire 2000–2009 time frame.[1] This growth included the continued coverage of reality programs that had already been part of *Us Weekly*'s content, such as the ongoing coverage of the cyclical celetoids of the *Bachelor/Bachelorette* franchise, which were featured in 23 main cover stories and 43 second-level cover stories, reaffirming this franchise's central place in *Us Weekly*'s gossip formula. But it was also spurred by the continued growth and success of the reality television genre itself, as the 2010s witnessed the expansion of existing franchises and the birth of new programs. The parallel growth of these two media forms reflects their symbiotic relationship, as the continued coverage in *Us Weekly* helped drive audiences to these programs while also increasing the range of celebrities the magazine could itself cover and cultivate.

For instance, the *Real Housewives* franchise, which launched in 2009 and was featured in only one main *Us Weekly* cover story in that year, grew the main franchise from four programs to seven between 2010 and 2011[2] and developed a whopping eleven spin-offs and specials between 2008 and 2014.[3] *Us Weekly*'s thirteen main cover stories and thirty-eight second-level cover stories dedicated to various *Housewives* between 2010 and 2014 both capitalized on the franchise's popularity and helped build it through coverage that included promotional narratives that explicitly drew audiences back to the narrative of the show and extended some cast members (particularly *Real Housewives of New York*'s Bethenny Frankel and *Real Housewives of New Jersey*'s Teresa Guidice, who together accounted for eleven of the thirteen *Housewives* main cover stories) into celebrities through coverage of their off-screen selves. *Us Weekly* also benefitted from a new crop of cast members to cover as a result of the emergence of new shows, such as the *Teen Mom* (2010–present) franchise, an MTV reality docusoap appealing to the same young female audiences as *The Hills*, which was featured in ten main cover stories and twenty-two second-level cover stories, and *Duck Dynasty* (2012–2017), which was featured in five main cover stories and five second-level cover stories. This consistent coverage of reality television was, in one view, tied to *Us Weekly*'s traditional role as an extratextual media source that looks to entertainment institutions to produce personalities for it to cover. At the same time, as argued throughout this book, *Us Weekly*'s coverage of reality television cast members also enabled it to grow its own celebrity, positioning the magazine as a vehicle for the rise of a more lasting form of reality celebrity—the extraordinarily ordinary celebrity—that moved the right kind of individuals outside of the narrative boundaries of the original reality television programs to more directly shape and benefit from the celebrity image.

Us Weekly's ongoing role as a vehicle for the production of the extraordinarily ordinary celebrity is perhaps best illustrated by its attention to the Kardashian family, who were by far the most covered reality television cast members in *Us Weekly* during the first five years of the 2010s, with forty-one main cover stories and seventy-four second-level cover stories devoted to at least one member of the family. To put this in context, while reality television cast members *overall* accounted for just 11 percent of the magazine's main cover stories between 2000 and 2009, coverage of the Kardashians alone accounted for 15 percent of *all* the main cover stories in *Us Weekly* between 2010 and 2014. Additionally, second-level cover stories featuring a Kardashian appeared nearly every month and typically multiple times per month. The attention to the family was so intense that some main story covers on one family member would be accompanied by a second-level cover story on a different Kardashian, thus increasing the family's overall centrality to the magazine's attention to celebrity culture (see fig. 7). These stories blended promotion narratives about current story lines on *Keeping Up with the Kardashians* or one of its related spin-offs or specials with coverage of

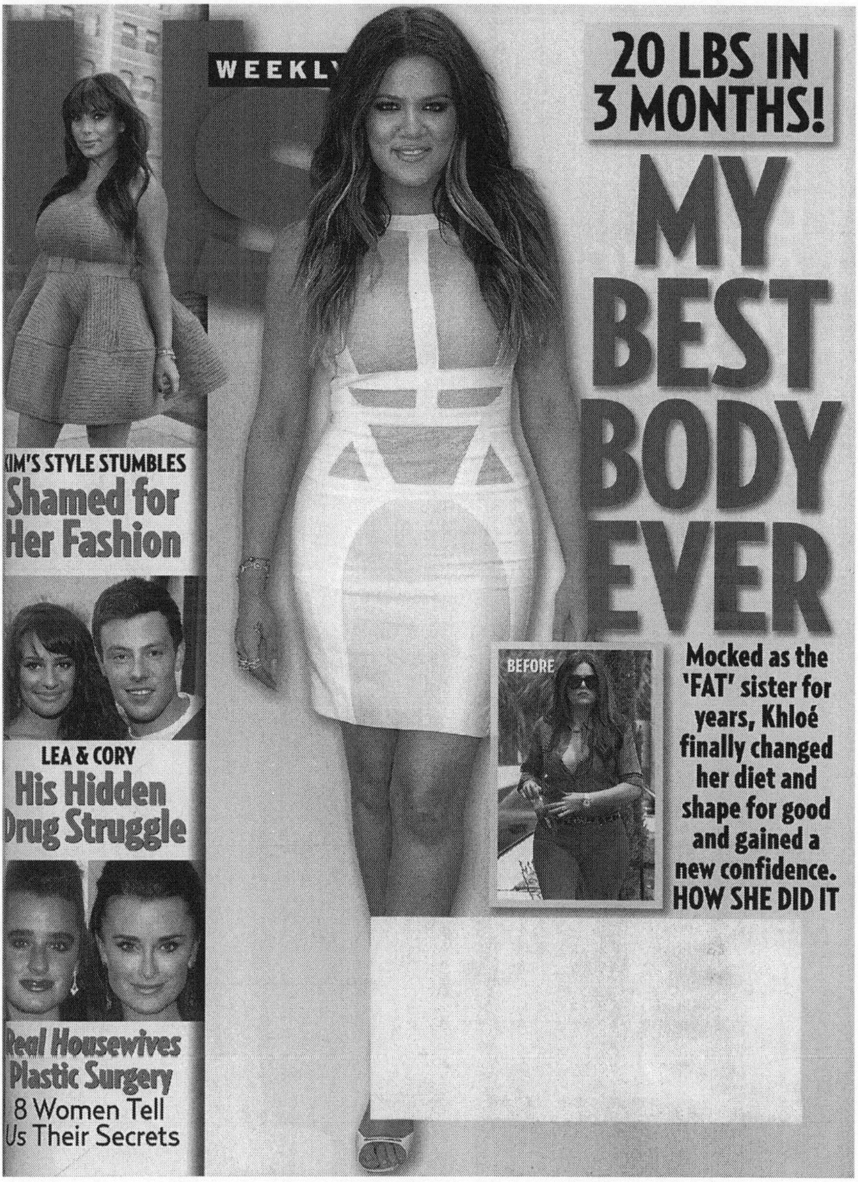

Figure 7. Multiple Kardashian cover stories, April 15, 2013.

the labor of ordinariness and celebrity lifestyle labor of the various family members outside of the show, helping to grow them into extraordinarily ordinary celebrities. For instance, figure 7 depicts the April 15, 2013, cover featuring Khloé Kardashian's "best body ever," framing her celebrity status around her possession of a conventionally attractive body and the "work" it took to get it. On the same cover, her sister Kim appears in a second-level cover story claiming she has been "shamed for her fashion," reinforcing the same emphasis on body and beauty that is a hallmark of the female celebrity, and, while negatively judging Kim's efforts in this performance of celerity lifestyle labor, it nevertheless reinforces that her body and beauty helped put her into the category of celebrity in the first place.

The increased coverage of the Kardashians, and indeed reality television celebrity more generally, speaks to *Us Weekly*'s continued power to shape, not simply respond to, the cultural zeitgeist in the twenty-first century. But the turn to reality television celebrity is also evidence of the ways in which print gossip weeklies had to pivot to maintain their relevance in a rapidly changing celebrity media market. The emergence of digital media as a space to engage with celebrity culture, including the rise of gossip blogs and other digital sources that offered immediate and interactive access to the latest gossip and the emergence of social media platforms that promised direct and frequent access to celebrities themselves, had a profound impact on the print gossip weekly market. The print media industry's decline began in the first decade of the twenty-first century, as discussed elsewhere in this book, and intensified in the 2010s. According to the *New York Times*, the once-robust celebrity gossip genre experienced some of the worst drops in newsstand sales of all print media in 2012, and *Us Weekly* itself was down 11.4 percent that year (Haughney, 2012, August 7). Given the importance of newsstand sales to the genre's overall circulation, such declines offered strong indications that audiences were turning elsewhere for their celebrity gossip. The magazine industry consultant John Harrington explicitly pointed to online sources' ability to offer quick and up-to-the-minute gossip as the impetus for this decline, saying, "By the time the magazine comes out, it's old news. We're on to the next scandal" (qtd. in ibid.). The trend continued throughout the decade, with the average newsstand sales for *Us Weekly* falling 16.7 percent in the first half of 2013 and declining an additional 15 percent in the first half of 2014, though, as usual, it fared better than competitors like *In Touch* (down 23.5 percent), *Star* (down 21.8 percent), and *Life & Style Weekly* (down 21.7 percent) (Kelly, 2013, October 2; Haughney, 2014, August 8).

Though far from the circulation numbers of its early 2000s golden age, *Us Weekly* remains the leader in print celebrity gossip weeklies and has, along with many of its competitors, also tapped into the digital gossip landscape with a successful web portal (usmagazine.com) and an active presence on social media platforms like Facebook (https://www.facebook.com/UsWeekly/), Twitter (@usweekly), and Instagram (@usweekly). I have argued throughout this book that the reliance on coverage of reality television cast members within its existing gossip formulas and the growth of extraordinarily ordinary celebrities were critical to its ability to remain a viable player during this moment of technological transition. Indeed, I have written elsewhere about the ways in which the same digital upstarts that threatened *Us Weekly*'s cultural dominance remain indebted to its legacy (Meyers, 2013). On a content level, gossip blogs certainly relied on *Us Weekly*'s existing coverage and the journalistic practices and access to celebrities that supported it as the springboard for the gossip commentary, rather than reporting, that comprised most of the popular blogs. More importantly, however, the photo-heavy style, the cheeky look at the real lives of celebrities, and the formulaic gossip narratives focused on body, beauty, and relationships established by the magazine provided the template for the tone and style adopted by celebrity gossip bloggers.

Beyond its influence on both print and digital gossip media, *Us Weekly*'s turn toward the ordinary as the nexus of fame is also echoed in the ways in which celebrities themselves have harnessed the tools of social media to produce and circulate their own images. For instance, Kim Kardashian, who certainly relied heavily on the coverage of her labor of ordinariness and celebrity lifestyle labor in *Us Weekly* and other gossip weeklies to build her persona beyond its reality television roots, further intensified her celebrity status through her savvy engagement of the same discourses on her personal social media platforms. Sharing "candid" photos of her everyday life and family alongside glamorous moments preparing for the red carpet or taking a luxury vacation, Kim offers audiences access to the same sort of offstage and private-focused self that was formerly the primary province of celebrity gossip weeklies like *Us Weekly*. In many ways, social media has become a new form of extratextual engagement with celebrity, working alongside or potentially even bypassing traditional extratextual sources.

For instance, in her book, *Bachelor Nation: Inside the World of America's Favorite Guilty Pleasure*, the *Los Angeles Times* media reporter Amy Kaufman (2018) posits that cast members on *The Bachelor/Bachelorette* now look to social media, more so than traditional media, to extend their celebrity beyond the show and even see being on the show as a path to getting followers—and the financial and social rewards that come from this form of microcelebrity—rather than as an end in itself. Instead of needing *Us Weekly* to cover their labors of ordinariness and celebrity lifestyle labors, these reality cast members harness the tools of social media to do it themselves, thus broadening the range of cast members who find some level of lasting celetoid- or microcelebrity-level fame beyond the program. Moreover, the related rise of celebrities *originating* on these platforms, such as Instagram Influencers or YouTube stars, further speaks to the ways in which the successful leveraging of ordinariness is used to construct celebrity. In contemporary digital culture, the work of growing your own celebrity is now a mode of neoliberal entrepreneurship in which the work of self-branding and leveraging one's identity is presented as a viable path to celebrity. Echoing the myth of meritocracy that has always underscored celebrity culture and was central to *Us Weekly*'s elevation of ordinary individuals into celebrity culture, the rise of social media celebrity suggests that any ordinary person can achieve fame simply by working hard and being herself, while obscuring the dominant norms that still limit who rises to the top.

Of course, celebrities are not the only ones with access to these platforms, and this work of being a celebrity—that presentational labor of constructing the self rooted in the blurring of private and public selves—is now also a central component of our everyday media and social lives within the digital age. According to Wilson (2014), "More and more, like reality television celebrities, we live our private lives in public forums such as Facebook and Twitter that require us to constantly negotiate between our 'true' and 'performed' selves, as well as those of others. . . . We circulate intimate glimpses into our personal identities and private lives that we imagine will please our audiences, while taking pleasure in judging the self-presentation of others, consuming the profiles of friends, family, and enemies as we do the celebrities on reality television" (p. 434). The increased importance of private-side discourses to the notion of fame and to everyday social life in these spaces reinforces the importance of just being yourself that was elevated by the rise of the extraordinarily ordinary celebrity in *Us Weekly.*

The Future of Us Weekly*: Extraordinarily Ordinary in the Age of Trump*

I have made the case throughout this book that the corporate ownership and editorial leadership of *Us Weekly* played a crucial role in its rise to the top of the celebrity weekly market and, more specifically, the development of the style, tone, and ideological approach that helped redefine celebrity culture. Recent industrial shifts around *Us Weekly* reaffirm the important roles celebrity culture and celebrity gossip continue to play in shaping social and political norms. As a struggling title in the early 2000s, the magazine was revived by Disney's co-ownership and its subsequent installation of Bonnie Fuller and then Janice Min as editor in chief. Riding high on *Us Weekly*'s dominance of the market, the co-owner Wenner Media borrowed heavily to regain full control of—and profits from—the magazine in 2006, just before the economic recession and subsequent collapse of the print media market. Though the magazine continued to perform better than competitors throughout the 2010s and helped shore up the bottom line of Wenner Media more generally, the pressure of outside forces soon became overwhelming. Under the weight of the debt it acquired to buy out Disney's shares and mounting financial challenges across its other titles (including the declining readership for its flagship magazine, *Rolling Stone*, and legal payments incurred as a result of defamation lawsuits in the wake of *Rolling Stone*'s widely condemned 2014 article detailing allegations of a gang rape at a University of Virginia fraternity), rumors began to circulate in 2016 that Wenner Media was looking for another buyer for its former cash cow to alleviate these financial burdens (Ember, 2017, March 16; Kelly, 2016, December 20).

Other print media powerhouses, including Tronc and Hearst Magazines, vied to purchase the title, indicating *Us Weekly*'s continued value even in a depressed print media market (Bloomgarden-Smoke and Steigrad, 2017, March 20). The sale was ultimately made to American Media Inc. (AMI), best known as the longtime publisher of supermarket tabloid the *National Enquirer*, for $100 million in March 2017 (ibid.). Unlike Wenner Media's purchase of the magazine from Disney that kept editorial leadership and style in place, AMI's takeover was accompanied by a round of layoffs that included nearly half of the editorial staff, as well as then editor in chief Michael Steele (who worked for years under Janice Min and took over when she departed in 2008) (Kelly, 2017, March 24). The CEO and chairman, David J. Pecker, assured the public that AMI would "ensure that *Us Weekly*'s distinct editorial voice continues to deliver the kind of celebrity news reporting that its millions of readers and business partners know and trust," but the shake-up at all editorial levels left many media watchers and loyal readers nervous about the future of the celebrity weekly (American Media Inc., 2017, April 25, para. 2; Weber & Finger, 2017, May 4).

The sale of the crown jewel of the celebrity weekly market to Pecker's AMI was a seismic shift in the gossip weekly market that has multiple industrial and social implications for the future of celebrity gossip. First, it was part of a larger consolidation of the gossip weekly market under the AMI umbrella. As of this writing, AMI is now the largest owner of celebrity gossip titles across the U.S. market. While the print gossip market may not be at the heights of the early 2000s, it remains a robust subgenre of the magazine market and a crucial player in the validation of mainstream celebrity culture. AMI already owned *Star* and *OK!* magazine, as well as the more down-market tabloid the *National Enquirer*, when it bought *Us Weekly* in 2017. In June 2018, it added *In Touch*, *Life & Style*, and *Closer* to its stable of celebrity weeklies when it bought those titles from Bauer Publications, making AMI the owner of "every large-scale celebrity magazine except [publishing competitor] Meredith's *People*, the No. 1 title in the market" (Kelly, 2018, June 15, para. 7). With these acquisitions, David Pecker and AMI have an unprecedented level of control over how celebrity culture is produced and circulated that is largely invisible to the everyday consumer.

Given the role of celebrities as anchors for cultural and political ideologies, this power is about more than just which celebrities rise to the top but the ideological meanings that rise along with them. The power of the gossip press and AMI in particular to shape public discourse about public figures was made particularly evident when, in August 2018, Pecker reached an immunity deal with federal prosecutors investigating potential campaign finance violations by the Donald Trump presidential campaign. As the longtime publisher of the *National Enquirer*, Pecker was already renowned for using that tabloid to circulate supportive coverage of Donald Trump. The *Enquirer* had a "cozy relationship" with Trump dating back to his days on *The Apprentice*, when any negative stories that would emerge about Trump were "dead on arrival," according to former employees, and it began supporting his presidential aspirations as far back as 2010 (Associated Press, 2018b, August 23). Indeed, in its first ever endorsement of a presidential candidate, the *National Enquirer* officially backed Trump's presidential candidacy in 2016 and continued to run positive and supportive stories about him alongside disparaging reports about his opponent, Hillary Clinton (ibid.). In his immunity deal, Pecker provided details regarding the *National Enquirer*'s "catch-and-kill" efforts to protect then presidential candidate Trump from the emergence of stories about extramarital affairs with Karen McDougal, a former Playboy model, and Stephanie Clifford, an adult-film star who performed under the name Stormy Daniels, by paying off the two women, possibly with the knowledge and financial support of the Trump campaign (Graves, 2018, August 23; Rutenberg, Ruiz, & Protess, 2018, August 23). Catch-and-kills are common tabloid industry practice of burying a scandal by buying exclusive rights to a story with the intention of preventing competitors from obtaining it and blocking those involved from selling it elsewhere rather than ever publishing it (Graves, 2018, August 23). They are an explicit example of the central role celebrity gossip media still play in shaping public discourse, as keeping such a glimpse of the celebrity's private life out of the news cycle helps control the meaning of his or her image. In this case, the revelation of these extramarital affairs and the payouts to the women that may have come from the Trump campaign could have potentially damaged his presidential aspirations at a critical time during the campaign. According to reports about Pecker's disclosures, AMI and the *National Enquirer* kept a safe "containing documents on hush money and other damaging stories" on Trump, as well as other celebrities (Associated Press, 2018a, August 23). The safe was "a source of great power for Pecker," according to sources close to AMI, allowing the company to "ingratiate itself with [celebrities by protecting their secrets] and ask for favors in return" (ibid.). While certainly not the only media source backing Trump's campaign or potentially benefitting from his rise to power, these revelations point to the crucial role played by a gossip tabloid—a media form often dismissed for its *lack* of political relevance—in the political fortunes of Donald Trump and the continued importance of celebrity gossip to social and political life.

Trump in Us Weekly

Given *Us Weekly*'s top position in the market and its greater cultural legitimacy in comparison to supermarket tabloid the *National Enquirer*, AMI's purchase of the title can be viewed as both an economic decision and as a way to extend and validate its ideological platform. Prior to the AMI sale, *Us Weekly* certainly covered Trump but primarily in his role as the host of *The Apprentice* rather than any other public or private exploits. Notably, he never appeared on the cover until after he announced his presidential candidacy, when a February 8, 2016, cover story featuring Trump and his wife, Melania, promised readers a glimpse of "life at home with the controversial candidate" (Grossbart, 2016, February 8, p. 40). Instead of directly focusing on Trump, who as a male celebrity would not be a typical focal point for *Us Weekly* coverage anyway, this article, titled "Donald's First Lady," was about Melania and included a sidebar piece ostensibly authored by her, titled "The Donald Only I Know," that offered readers a glimpse of the real family behind the political headlines. While this focus on his family life helped to humanize Trump as "just like *Us!*," this singular cover story was hardly part of a larger campaign by the magazine to promote his candidacy. No other cover story on Trump or his family was run during the campaign, and *Us Weekly* also ran a Hillary Clinton cover on May 2, 2016, touting "25 things you don't know" about the Democratic nominee, suggesting editors were tapping into a broader public interest in the personas of the candidates rather than using the magazine to advocate for their politics. Shortly after Trump was elected president, *Us Weekly* ran its second ever cover story on a Trump family member, offering a glimpse inside "Melania's Private World" (December 19, 2016). In keeping with the themes that dominate *Us Weekly*, the article stressed that despite her new place on the political mainstage as the First Lady, she "has to pick her son up at school" and that thirteen-year-old Barron "is the priority for now" (Andersson, 2016, December 19, p. 49). Again, such coverage of presidential families was not unprecedented, as *Us* had previously devoted several covers to the Obama family during Barack Obama's presidency (including June 30, 2008; November 11, 2008; and February 2, 2009). The presence of Trump and his family in *Us Weekly* at this point, prior to the AMI sale, is consistent with its existing more limited coverage of political celebrity.

However, coverage of the Trump family suddenly increased in early 2017, with a run of five consecutive main cover stories between January 30 (with an on-sale date that coincided with Trump's January 20, 2017, inauguration) and February 27 that featured either Melania or Trump's daughter, Ivanka. It is worth noting that there was no comparable run of consecutive covers devoted to the Obama family during his presidency and no covers at all devoted to George W. Bush and his family during his presidency. According to the *New York Post* media critic Keith J. Kelly (2017, February 10), industry insiders attributed this increase in coverage as a move by Jann Wenner "to curry favor with Pecker, an unabashed Donald Trump supporter," as he sought to close the deal to sell the magazine. But Kelly also notes that the covers were selling well, with the first three issues of this run driving up newsstand sales for *Us Weekly* by 40 percent (ibid.). Just as *Us Weekly* cashed in on the rising popularity of reality television, it here appeared to tap into the popular interest in the new president and his family as a way to sell magazines. However, given *Us Weekly*'s long-standing efforts to drive the zeitgeist rather than simply respond to it and the ongoing behind-the-scenes negotiations between Wenner Media and AMI, it appears that this was more than simply a response to audience desires. *Us Weekly* cover stories both create and respond to reader demand, earning profits for the magazine while simultaneously helping to shape the image of those celebrities covered. This Trump coverage was not universally sycophantic, but it overwhelmingly worked to paint the family and the administration in a more positive light in ways that fit with AMI's other Trump coverage.

The shift in the tone of coverage of Trump and his family continued and indeed intensified after AMI took over the magazine in March 2017. For instance, the June 19, 2017, cover featured Ivanka declaring, "Why I disagree with my dad," in the wake of Trump's decision to withdraw from the Paris Agreement, part of the global effort to fight climate change, and seemed to offer a critique of President Trump's political policies as a means to define the real Ivanka to readers. The piece frames Ivanka as a "calming influence" who works to influence her father's policies on more liberal issues like climate change, women's issues, and LGBTQ rights by using her role as "beloved daughter . . . [who] he listens to more than anyone" (Ivanka Trump: Standing tall in Washington, 2017, June 19, p. 53). The article again humanizes Trump by tying him to his family and reassures more liberal readers that Ivanka is just like us and will protect more liberal interests during her father's presidency. Thus, in contrast to the political reality in which the Trump administration continues to dismantle laws and policies in these areas, *Us Weekly* uses its position as a more respectable source of the truth behind the (political) celebrity facade to construct and circulate a different and more positive image of the president. With AMI's total dominance of the celebrity weekly market combined with the admitted use of catch-and-kills to protect and/or coerce celebrities, there is little space to challenge the narratives and norms expressed, and Pecker has the power to shape celebrity culture as he sees fit.

Conclusion

Celebrity weeklies have long served as key sites for the performance of labor of ordinariness, and *Us Weekly*'s increased coverage of reality cast members explicitly draws on discourses of authenticity and realness, elevating the ordinary self already on display in reality television into the more rarefied realm of celebrity culture. If celebrities are always already the markers of normative values of gender, race, and class in contemporary society, by elevating ordinariness as the core of celebrity, *Us Weekly* helped define exactly what sort of ordinary self matters in contemporary society. Furthermore, by combining the labor of ordinariness with the celebrity lifestyle labor associated with contemporary celebrity culture, *Us Weekly* helped transform them from merely ordinary to extraordinarily ordinary through a gendered appeal to consumption as a means to define the self. Being the right kind of self to merit celebrity and the social and economic values attached to that identity is thus achieved by looking, acting, and, most importantly, consuming in the right sort of way, reinscribing dominant norms of identity even as the shift toward ordinariness appears to open up and diversify the range of identities that matter. As the discourses established within *Us Weekly*'s attention to extraordinarily ordinary celebrity intensify with the rise of digital and social media, the allure of celebrity culture becomes less that celebrities are just like us and more that we are, or at least can be, just like them.

ACKNOWLEDGMENTS

I would like to thank the staff at the Ray and Pat Browne Popular Culture Library at Bowling Green State University, particularly Stefanie Hunker and Dana Nemeth, for helping me navigate the *Us Weekly* archive and create my digital archive for this project. Thanks also to the ladies of the "Back Channel" for always being a sounding board, for the laughs, and for the picture parades during the writing phase of this project. Thanks to the Communication and Journalism Department Research Group for their feedback as this project was taking shape. Special thanks to Kathy Battles, Brooke Edge, Amanda Klein, Alice Leppert, and Faye Woods for their thoughtful and constructive critiques of early drafts of chapters. Thank you to Dema Iskander for her help finalizing the manuscript and dealing with my citations. Finally, thank you to my family for their love and support.

NOTES

INTRODUCTION

1. *Star* was originally a newsprint tabloid whose celebrity coverage was less sophisticated and more tawdry than a typical celebrity weekly. However, former *Us Weekly* editor Bonnie Fuller took over the title in 2003 and transformed it into a glossy magazine format that mimicked the formula she introduced at *Us Weekly*.

2. Even this archive, however, is not totally complete. According to the Bowling Green State University library catalog, the archive is missing the following issues: February 5, 2001; July 2, 2001; August 12–December 25, 2001; September 12, 2005; and the entire volume for July–November 2012. I searched for these missing issues online to at least see the cover images for analysis. *Us Weekly* does not maintain a complete online archive (though does have covers from the years 2010–2014 available on its online portal usweekly.com), and, as mentioned above, most digital library access is restricted to text only. While I was unable to locate all of the issues, a few were available for purchase through sites like ebay.com and included cover images. Given that most of the missing issues from the early 2000s were from 2001, which was prior to Fuller/Min's editorial leadership and the magazine's shift to reality television coverage, these absences do not negatively affect my overall analysis.

3. This full archive was assembled for the years 2000–2009, the primary time frame of this study. For the years 2010–2017, only covers and any full-length articles featuring the Trump family were collected.

CHAPTER 1 — THE ORDINARY AND THE EXTRAORDINARY

1. Paris Hilton offers a similarly liminal case that reveals the difficulty of defining celebrity broadly and opens space for future research on the complexity of the extraordinarily ordinary celebrity specifically. She did appear in a popular reality program, *The Simple Life* (2003–2007), and also appeared frequently in the pages of *Us Weekly* during the time of my study. But I chose not to include her in my analysis because her fame is not attached to her reality program in the same way as Kim's (or other reality celebrities used throughout the book). Though she is not an achieved celebrity in the ways that Ozzy

Osbourne or Jessica Simpson can claim, I argue Hilton's complex celebrity image touches on reality television ordinariness but is not rooted in it. She is certainly a good example of the type of celetoid decried as famous for being famous, but the interplay of extraordinary and ordinary in her image is outside the scope of this research (see Sconce, 2007).

2. The role of Spencer and Heidi on *The Hills* and its relevance to both their stardom and that of *Hills* costar Lauren Conrad will be discussed in greater detail in chapter 4.

CHAPTER 2 — THE LABOR OF ORDINARINESS

1. Turner is not here using Rojek's term "achieved celebrity," which grounds fame in talent, but rather is referring simply to the act of acquiring fame by an ordinary individual.

2. Cast members from the predominantly African American cast of *The Real Housewives of Atlanta* have more recently appeared in both main and second-level cover stories (e.g., a cover story featuring Nene Leakes appeared on November 26, 2012), but this occurred after the time frame of this study.

3. *Joe Millionaire* was a reality-competition dating program in which twenty women competed for the affections of a man, Evan Marriott, they believed had recently inherited $50 million but who was actually a broke working-class construction worker from Florida. The audience was in on the deception from the beginning, and the conceit was to see which female contestants were authentically "in love" with Marriott and which were gold diggers, who were only interested in his (nonexistent) money.

4. Marriott, notably, had a slightly longer run as a celetoid due to his tie to discourses of fame damage, as will be discussed in chapter 3.

5. A more detailed discussion of the attention celebrity lifestyle labor in this article appears in chapter 3.

6. This season did not end in a proposal, as many subsequent seasons have done, in accordance with the romance narrative of the program. The couple dated briefly but broke up shortly after the finale.

7. Though Min stated that Firestone was the first *Bachelor* star to appear on the cover, my research indicates that the bachelor Aaron Buerge was actually the first, appearing on the November 25, 2002, cover in the lead up to the season 2 finale. Furthermore, the show had already been covered by the magazine to some degree since season 1 (see discussion earlier in this chapter), including increased coverage during Firestone's season prior to his cover appearance. This may have also been Wenner's idea, but nevertheless, the franchise was already establishing a clear place in *Us Weekly*'s gossip formulas prior to Firestone's allegedly top-selling postfinale interview cover.

8. *The Bachelor* and *The Bachelorette* finish filming prior to the airing of the season, but the cast members are forbidden to reveal any specific details about how the season progresses.

9. For an overview of *Bachelor*/*Bachelorette* covers during 2003–2018, see https://www.usmagazine.com/entertainment/pictures/bachelor-us-weekly-covers-2014247/

10. While the couple's postseason narrative was short-lived, they did briefly re-emerge at the end of 2007 in a second-level cover story detailing the "Bachelor Blow-Up" in which Delgado was arrested for hitting Velnick after an argument (Andersson, 2007, December 10). Though charges were later dropped, the minimal subsequent coverage of the couple marked them as outside of the fairy-tale narrative of the franchise, and they broke up for good in December 2009.

11. See chapter 3 for further discussion of Trista's celebrity lifestyle labor and its role in constructing her extraordinarily ordinary celebrity status.

CHAPTER 3 — CELEBRITY LIFESTYLE LABOR

1. As discussed in chapter 2, Schefft's initial emergence on reality television was as a cast member and eventual winner of *The Bachelor* in 2003 when Andrew Firestone gave her the final rose (see Youngman, 2003).

2. Rob and Amber, both former *Survivor* castaways, met during the filming of *Survivor: All-Stars*. While their relationship and eventual wedding were an important part of their celebrity images, it is important to recognize that, this coupling, unlike those connected to the *Bachelor* franchise, was not an intended outcome of the program narrative.

3. The first ever appearance of reality television cast members on the cover occurred when the final five contestants from the first seasons of *Survivor*, including Hatch, appeared on the cover of the August 21, 2000, issue. This cover featured head shots of the final contestants from the show superimposed over an aerial shot of the *Survivor* island and the headline "WHO WILL WIN?," thus keeping the focus on the program itself, not the specific individuals emerging from it. In contrast, the cover photo of Hatch was shot specifically for the magazine and features him smiling playfully at the camera in a well-tailored suit with his shirt open to the waist (calling up his frequent nakedness on the show), clearly positioning him as a celebrity, not just a contestant on the show.

4. While Nick Lachey and Jessica Simpson did have a successful reality television program, *Newlyweds: Nick & Jessica* (2003–2005), they were already established pop singers at the time of the program. Thus, while reality television certainly helped bolster their fame, their initial fame was not tied to reality television. I have elsewhere explored the use of reality television by existing celebrities, but the focus of this project is on reality television as the initial site of public performance for a celebrity (Meyers, 2010; Meyers, 2013). A clear definition of celebrities who are studied here is available in chapter 1.

5. My analysis of the magazine identified seven consecutive covers devoted to the Gosselin scandal. Vincinguerra here is likely referring to these and simply misremembered the total number.

CHAPTER 4 — LAUREN CONRAD

1. See https://www.usmagazine.com/entertainment/pictures/bachelor-us-weekly-covers-2014247/39639-2/ for an overview of *Bachelor* franchise covers from 2003 to 2016.

2. Lauren appeared on *The Hills* from 2006 to 2009, leaving in the middle of season 5. She did return for the finale episode in 2010. She notably did not join the cast of the series revival, *The Hills: New Beginnings*, which began airing on MTV in June 2019 (Longeretta, 2018).

3. This time frame coincides with seasons 3 and 4 of *The Hills*, which were the last two full seasons that featured Lauren as the main lead for the show. Season 3 was also the highest rated season overall and included the most viewed episode of the series on March 24, 2008 (Stelter, 2008).

4. During the break between season 2 (which concluded on April 2, 2007) and season 3 (which premiered on August 13, 2007), rumors emerged in gossip media about the existence of a sex tape featuring Lauren and her ex-boyfriend Jason Whaler, including a second-level cover story in *Us Weekly* featuring Lauren and the headline "*The Hills* War: My Side of the Story," which came out just in time for the season 3 premiere. In the accompanying article,

Lauren and Whaler both vehemently denied the existence of said tape, and Lauren accused the series villains, Spencer Pratt and Heidi Montag, of fabricating and circulating rumors about a tape to hurt her reputation (Guarente, 2007, August 13). This heightened the existing feud between Lauren and Heidi, and the fallout from the sex tape rumors became a major plot point of season 3 of *The Hills*, as well as fodder for subsequent *Us Weekly* stories on both women.

5. The remaining *Hills* cover, on June 29, 2009, featured Stephanie Pratt, who had just been promoted from recurring cast member to main cast member in the wake of Lauren's departure at the end of season 5.

6. The inauthenticity of Heidi's image is certainly wrapped up in her multiple plastic surgeries, particularly in contrast to Lauren's "natural" beauty. While her first admitted surgeries, a nose job and breast implants, were the subject of her first solo cover on October 8, 2007, she is well known for having undergone ten plastic surgeries in one day in late 2009, a fact that was not revealed to the public until a *People* magazine cover on January 25, 2010, and is thus outside of the time frame of this analysis.

CONCLUSION

1. As with the primary archive for this book, these covers were accessed at the Ray and Pat Browne Popular Culture Library at Bowling Green State University. The archives for these years was incomplete, as it was missing all issues from July 2 to November 5, 2012. However, usweekly.com published a year-ending "Year in *Us Weekly*" overview of all covers for each year between 2010 and 2014, so I was able to fill in the missing issues. This yearly cover roundup was discontinued after 2014. The 2012 cover roundup is available here: https://www.usmagazine.com/celebrity-news/pictures/the-year-in-us-weekly-2012-20122611/26441/

2. The franchise included *The Real Housewives of Orange County* (2006–present), *The Real Housewives of New York City* (2008–present), *The Real Housewives of Atlanta* (2008–present), *The Real Housewives of New Jersey* (2009–present), *The Real Housewives of D.C.* (2010), *The Real Housewives of Beverly Hills* (2010–present), and *The Real Housewives of Miami* (2010–2013).

3. *Date My Ex: Jo & Slade* (2008), *Bethenny Ever After* (2010–2012), *Boys to Manzo* (2011), *Don't Be Tardy* (2012–present), *Havana Elsa* (2012), *The Kandi Factory* (2013), *Vanderpump Rules* (2013–present), *Tamra's OC Wedding* (2013), *I Dream of NeNe: The Wedding* (2013), *Kandi's Wedding* (2014), and *Manzo'd with Children* (2014–2016).

REFERENCES

Adweek staff (2005, March 14). Brad or Britney? Britney or Brad? It's 9 o'clock. *Adweek*. Retrieved June 18, 2018, from https://www.adweek.com/brand-marketing/brad-or-britney-britney-or-brad-its-9-oclock-78321/

Abrahamson, R. P. (2006, April 17). Kristin: Still copying Jess! *Us Weekly*, p. 38.

Abramowitz, R. (2009, July 22). Janice Min helped *Us Weekly* feed a hunger for celebrity. *Los Angeles Times*. Retrieved June 5, 2018, from http://articles.latimes.com/2009/jul/22/entertainment/et-usweekly22

Adams, R. (2012, February 8). Hot covers! One prince, three sisters, lots of breakups. *Wall Street Journal*, p. D1.

Affuso, E. (2009). "Don't just watch it, live it"—technology, corporate partnerships and *The Hills*. *Jump Cut, 51*. Retrieved from http://www.ejumpcut.org/archive/jc51.2009/Hills-Affuso/index.html

Age face-off! (2008, July 28). *Us Weekly*, 40.

Agresti, A. (2006, October 9). This minute you want to know about . . . *The Bachelor*'s real prince. *US Weekly*, 80.

Agresti, A. (2007, June 4). LC's dress decision! *Us Weekly*, 49.

Agresti, A. (2008, April 28). Celebrity designer of the year: Lauren Conrad. *Us Weekly*, 70–71.

Agresti, A. (2008, May 19). The feud gets worse. *Us Weekly*, 58–63.

Agresti, A. (2008, December 15). Her mom's fury. *Us Weekly*, 42–47.

Agresti, A., Andersson, E., Bartolomeo, J., Cina, M., Guarente, G., & O'Neill, J. (2007, October 2). Power players 2007. *Us Weekly*, 80–93.

American Media Inc. (2017, April 25). American Media, Inc. finalizes purchase of *Us Weekly*. [Press release]. Retrieved from https://www.americanmediainc.com/press-release/american-media-inc-finalizes-purchase-us-weekly

America's Dairy Farmers and Milk Processors. (2001, May 21). Got Milk? [Advertisement]. *Us Weekly*, 27.

Andersson, E. (2007, December 10). *Bachelor* couple blowup. *Us Weekly*, 76–77.

Andersson, E. (2016, December 19). Inside Melania's world. *Us Weekly*, 48–51.

Andrejevic, M. (2002). The kinder, gentler gaze of *Big Brother*: Reality TV in the era of digital capitalism. *New Media & Society, 4*(2), 251–270.

Andrejevic, M. (2004). *Reality TV: The work of being watched*. Lanham, MD: Rowman & Littlefield.

Appel, D., Baker, K., & Vituscka, J. (2007, November 12). Lauren's search for love. *Us Weekly*, 58–63.

Associated Press. (2018a, August 23). A *National Enquirer* safe is said to have held damaging Trump stories. *The Los Angeles Times*. Retrieved from http://www.latimes.com/politics/la-na-pol-national-enquirer-trump-vault-20180823-story.html

Associated Press. (2018b, August 23). *Enquirer*-Trump ties go way beyond tabloid fodder. *CBS News*. Retrieved from https://www.cbsnews.com/news/enquirer-trump-ties-go-way-beyond-tabloid-fodder/

Baker, K., & Coats, C. (2003, February 17). *Joe Millionaire*: Sarah on her secret past. *Us Weekly*, 10–11.

Barnhart, A. (2010, December 6). How reality TV took over primetime. *The Kansas City Star*. Retrieved from http://www.kansascity.com/entertainment/tv/article311105/How-reality-TV-took-over-prime-time.html

Bartolomeo, J. (2003, January 27). Oh boy! *The Bachelorette*: Trista's choices. *Us Weekly*, 58.

Bartolomeo, J. (2003, September 8). Trista & Ryan's fantasy wedding! *Us Weekly*, 44–47.

Bartolomeo, J. (2004, February 23). Andrew & Jen reunited! *Us Weekly*, 52.

Bartolomeo, J. (2004, April 26) *The Apprentice*'s Bill & *The Bachelor*'s Jen Hot New Love! *Us Weekly*, 60–61.

Bartolomeo, J. (2004, May 3). Has Andrew Lost Jen Forever? *Us Weekly*, 46–50.

Bartolomeo, J. (2004, June 21). Meredith's wedding dress. *Us Weekly*, 68–69.

Bartolomeo, J. (2004, December 27). Jen Schefft finds love! *Us Weekly*, 50–53.

Bartolomeo, J. (2005, March 14). Jen Schefft talks: Why Jerry wasn't the one. *Us Weekly*, 107.

Bartolomeo, J., & Dirmann, T. (2004, December 13). *The Bachelor*'s Byron & Mary: "We're getting married!" *Us Weekly*, 68–69.

Bartolomeo, J. Mehalic, J., & Reinstein, M. (2007, May 7). Style winners: 7 in '07. *Us Weekly*, 78–81.

Becker, A. (2006, October 17). *Flavor of Love* tops the charts. *Broadcasting & Cable*. Retrieved from https://www.broadcastingcable.com/news/flavor-love-tops-charts-29626

Berger, L. (2016, July). Lauren Conrad serves it up. *Redbook*, 116–122.

Biressi, A., & Nunn, H. (2004). The especially remarkable: Celebrity and social mobility in reality TV. *Medactive, 2*(2), 44–58.

Bloomgarden-Smoke, K., & Steigrad, A. (2017, March 20). *Us Weekly* layoffs said to start next week. *Women's Wear Daily*. Retrieved from https://wwd.com/business-news/media/us-weekly-layoffs-rumored-to-start-next-week-10847996/

Bonner, F. (2003). *Ordinary television*. London, UK, & Thousand Oaks, CA: Sage.

Boorstin, D. J. (1964). *The image: A guide to pseudo-events in America*. New York, NY: Harper & Row.

Bromley, M. (2008, October 13). *Us* fashion roundtable. *Us Weekly*, 74–77.

Bruce, L. (2007, April 16). Secrets of *The Hills*. *Us Weekly*, 78–79.

Burston, C. (2009, August 24). Teens rock the house! *Us Weekly*, 34–35.

Carr, D. (2003, July 23). Formula receives credit as Us Weekly picks editor. *The New York Times*, p. C2.

Carr, D. (2008, June 29). 101 secrets (and 9 lives) of a magazine star. *The New York Times*. Retrieved from https://www.nytimes.com/2008/06/29/business/media/29bonnie.html

Carter, B. (2003, January 25). Reality shows alter way TV does business: Real winners. *The New York Times*, pp. A1, C14.

Cina, M. (2007, January 22). Celebrity beach don'ts. *Us Weekly*. 68–69.

Colford, P. D. (2001, February 28). *Us Weekly* is taking celeb coverage to Disney's land. *New York Daily News*, p. 24.

Collins, S. (2002, October 11–13). For nets, it's midweek mayhem. *Hollywood Reporter*, 1, 65.

Collins, S. (2008). Making the most out of 15 minutes: Reality TV's dispensable celebrity. *Television & New Media*, *9(2)*, 87–110.

Couldry, N. (2002). Playing for celebrity: *Big Brother* as ritual event. *Television & New Media*, *3*(3), 283–293.

Couldry, N. (2003). *Media rituals: A Critical Approach*. London, UK: Routledge.

Crupi, A. (2009, June 29). Keeping tabs on John & Kate. *Ad Week*. Retrieved from https://www.adweek.com/brand-marketing/keeping-tabs-john-kate-99719/

Curnutt, H. (2011) Durable participants: A generational approach to reality TV's "ordinary" labor pool. *Media, Culture & Society*, *33*(7), 1061–1076.

Currid-Halkett, E. (2010). *Starstruck: The business of celebrity*. New York, NY: Faber and Faber, Inc.

Davis, C. (2007, November 26). Hot Pics! *Us Weekly*, 26–27.

Davis, C. (2008, August 11). Matt & Shayne: Why they split. *Us Weekly*, 66–67.

DeCordova, R. (1991). *Picture personalities: The emergence of the star system in America*. Urbana, IL: University of Illinois Press.

Deely, H., Marchese, S., McColgin, C., & Schutte, L. (2008, April 7). Hollywood trend watch. *Us Weekly*, 84–85.

Deller, R. A. (2016). Star image, celebrity reality television and the fame cycle. *Celebrity Studies*,*7*(3), 373–389.

Dubrofsky, R. E. (2006). *The Bachelor*: Whiteness in the harem. *Critical Studies in Media Communication*, *23*(1), 39–56.

Dyer, R. (1986). *Heavenly bodies: Film stars and society*. Basingstoke, UK: Macmillan.

Dyer, R. (1998). *Stars* (New ed.). London, UK: BFI Publishing.

Ember, S. (2017, March 16). Us Weekly is sold to publisher of National Enquirer, reportedly for $100 million. *The New York Times*, p. B3.

Fairclough, K. (2008). Fame is a losing game: Celebrity gossip blogging, bitch culture and postfeminism, *Genders*, *48*. Retrieved from https://www.colorado.edu/genders archive1998-2013/2008/10/01/fame-losing-game-celebrity-gossip-blogging-bitch-culture-and-postfeminism

Fine, J. (2000, July 3). Worried Wenner goes to Plan B as "US" struggles. *Advertising Age*, *71*(28), 1.

Fine, J. (2003, February 24). "Us Weekly," "Yoga Journal" saw circulation soar in 2002. *Advertising Age*, *74*(8), 16.

Fine, J. (2004, October 25). Magazine of the year: *Us Weekly*. *Advertising Age*, *75*(43), s1–s6.

Firestone, A. (2003, April 7). Bachelor's Diary. *Us Weekly*, 84.

Fitzpatrick, M. (2016, February 2). A history of black contestants on *The Bachelor* and *The Bachelorette*. *Splinter*. Retrieved from https://splinternews.com/a-history-of-black-contestants-on-the-bachelor-and-the-1793854495

Fresh faces of 2006. (2006, October 2). *Us Weekly*, 80–85.

Frutkin, A. J. (2004, March 22). A who's who of reality television. *Mediaweek*, 20–25.

Gallo, J. (2003, March 17). Meet Bachelor No. 3. *Us Weekly*, 46.

Gamson, J. (1992). The assembly line of greatness: celebrity in twentieth-century America. *Critical Studies in Mass Communication, 9*, 1–24.

Gamson, J. (1994). *Claims to fame: Celebrity in contemporary America*. Berkeley, CA: University of California Press.

Gamson, J. (2011). The unwatched life is not worth living: The elevation of the ordinary in celebrity culture. *PMLA, 126*(4), 1061–1069.

Geraghty, C. (2000). Re-examining stardom: Questions of texts, bodies and performance. In C.

Gledhill & L. Williams (Eds.), *Reinventing film studies* (pp. 183–201). London: Arnold.

Gill, R. (2007). Postfeminist media culture: Elements of a sensibility. *European Journal of Cultural Studies, 10*(2), 147–166.

Graves, L. (2018, August 23). David Pecker, the tabloid king: Meet Trump's friend and fixer. *The Guardian*. Retrieved from https://www.theguardian.com/media/2018/aug/06/david-pecker-donald-trump-national-enquirer-profile

Grindstaff, L. (2011). Just be yourself—only more so: Ordinary celebrity in the era of self-service television. In M. M. Kraidy & K. Sender (Eds.), *The politics of reality television: Global perspectives* (pp. 44–57). London, UK, & New York, NY: Routledge.

Grindstaff, L. (2014). DI(t)Y, reality-style: The cultural work of ordinary celebrity. In L. Ouellette (Ed.), *A companion to reality television* (pp. 324–344). Malden, MA: John Wiley & Sons.

Grossbart, S. (2016, February 8). Melanie Trump: Donald's first lady. *Us Weekly*, 40–45.

Guarente, G. (2007, August 13). Lauren's side of the story. *Us Weekly*, 68–73.

Haralovich, M. B., & Trosset, M. W. (1992). Reality games: narrative pleasure and uncertainty in Survivor. In S. Murray and L. Ouelette (Eds.), *Reality TV: Remaking television culture* (pp. 72–96). New York, NY: New York City Press.

Hargraves, H. (2018). "For the first time in ______ history . . .": Microcelebrity and/as historicity in reality TV competitions. *Celebrity Studies, 9*(4), 503–518.

Haughney, C. (2012, August 7). Women's magazines lead overall decline in newsstand sales. *The New York Times*. Retrieved from https://mediadecoder.blogs.nytimes.com/2012/08/07/womens-magazines-lead-overall-decline-in-newsstand-sales/

Haughney, C. (2014, August 8). Celebrity magazine sales plummet on newsstands. *The New York Times*. Retrieved from https://www.nytimes.com/2014/08/08/business/media/newsstand-sales-of-celebrity-magazines-decline.html

Hayes, D. (2001, February 28). Disney takes stake in *Us Weekly* mag. *Daily Variety*, p. 6.

Hill, A. (2005). *Reality TV: Audiences and popular factual television*. New York, NY: Routledge.

Hill, A. (2015). *Reality TV*. New York, NY: Routledge.

Holmes, S. (2004a). "All you've got to worry about is the task, having a cup of tea, and doing a bit of sunbathing:" Approaching celebrity in *Big Brother*. In S. Holmes & D. Jermyn (Eds.), *Understanding reality television* (pp. 111–135). New York, NY: Routledge.

Holmes, S. (2004b). "Reality goes pop!": Reality TV, popular music, and narratives of stardom in *Pop Idol*. *Television & New Media, 5*(2), 147–172.

Holmes, S. (2005). "Off-guard, unkempt, unready"?: Deconstructing contemporary celebrity in *heat* magazine. *Continuum, 19*(1), 21–38.

Holmes, S., & Redmond, S. (2006). *Framing celebrity: New directions in celebrity culture*. London, UK: Routledge.

Hot pics. (2008, July 28). *Us Weekly*, 30.

Hot stuff: Heidi & Spencer engaged! (2007, June 11). *Us Weekly*, 58.

How to: Day-to-night dresses. (2008, July 28). *Us Weekly*, 86–87.

Ivanka Trump: Standing tall in Washington. (2017, June 19). *Us Weekly*, 50–53.

Ives, N. (2007, February 12). Going ga-ga over gossip: Celeb mags still soaring. *Advertising Age*, pp. 4–5.

Ives, N. (2007, April 9). Guess who's not getting any fatter! Celeb mags max out. *Advertising Age*, 78, 1.

Jones, O., & Pappas, B. (2000, August 21). Who's left. *Us Weekly*, 57–63.

Kaufman, A. (2018). *"Bachelor" nation: Inside the world of America's favorite guilty pleasure*. New York, NY: Penguin.

Kavka, M. (2012). *Reality TV*. Edinburgh, UK: Edinburgh University Press.

Kelly, K. J. (2011, May 13). Celeb mags' royal flush. *The New York Post*. Retrieved from https://nypost.com/2011/05/13/celeb-mags-royal-flush/

Kelly, K. J. (2013, October 2). Media ink: Brown in a new round of Newsweek axings. *The New York Post*, p. 26.

Kelly, K. J. (2014, July 4). Media ink: Wenner son also rises in empire shake-up. *The New York Post*, p. 22.

Kelly, K. J. (2016, December 20). Media ink: Wenner media head interested in selling *Us Weekly*. *The New York Post*. Retrieved from https://nypost.com/2016/12/20/wenner-media-head-interested-in-selling-us-weekly/

Kelly, K. J. (2017, February 10). Media ink: Wenner prez pitch mag's Trump focus reflects Pecker sale hopes. *The New York Post*, p. 28.

Kelly, K. J. (2017, March 24). Media ink: Pecker swinging ax 38 *Us Weekly* staffers pink-slipped. *The New York Post*, p. 24.

Kelly, K. J. (2018, June 15). Media ink: AMI's $80M deal continues big consolidation in magazine industry. *The New York Post*. Retrieved from https://nypost.com/2018/06/15/amis-80m-deal-continues-big-consolidation-in-magazine-industry/

Khamis, S., Ang, L., & Welling, R. (2017). Self-branding, "micro-celebrity" and the rise of social media influencers. *Celebrity Studies, 8*(2), 191–208.

Kilborn, R. (2003). *Staging the real: Factual TV programming in the age of "Big Brother."* Manchester, UK: Manchester University Press.

Kissell, R. (2000, August 25). An eye-land paradise: CBS sets summer record with socko "Survivor." *Daily Variety*, p. 1.

Klein, A. (2009). Postmodern marketing, Generation Y and the multiplatform viewing experience of MTV's *The Hills*. *Jump Cut* 51. Retrieved from http://www.ejumpcut.org/archive/jc51.2009/HillsKlein/index.html

Kompare, D. (2004). Extraordinarily ordinary: *The Osbournes* as "an American family." In S. Murray and L. Ouelette (Eds.), *Reality TV: Remaking television culture* (pp. 97–118). New York, NY: New York City Press.

Kozer, S. (as told to Gornstein, L). (2003, March 17). *Joe Millionaire*: Sarah bites back! *Us Weekly*, 6.

Kuczynski, A. (1999, September 27). Striking back at the empire: Wenner Media takes on the mighty Time Inc. in transforming Us to a monthly magazine. *The New York Times*. Retrieved from https://www.nytimes.com/1999/09/27/business/striking-back

-empire-wenner-media-takes-mighty-time-transforming-us-monthly.html?pagewanted=all

Kuczynski, A. (2001, February 28). Disney to take 50% stake in Us Weekly magazine. *The New York Times*, p. C1.

Lauren Conrad's fashion diary. (2007, February 26). *Us Weekly*, 78–79.

Leppert, A. (2015). *Keeping Up with the Kardashians*: Fame work and the production of entrepreneurial sisterhood. In E. Levine (Ed.), *Cupcakes, Pinterest, and ladyporn feminized popular culture in the early twenty-first century*. Urbana, IL: University of Illinois Press.

Leppert, A., & Wilson, J. (2008). Living *The Hills* life: Lauren Conrad as reality star, soap opera heroine, and brand. *Genders*, 48. Retrieved from https://www.colorado.edu/gendersarchive1998-2013/2008/07/02/living-hills-life-lauren-conrad-reality-star-soap-opera-heroine-and-brand

Levin, G. (2003, February 18). For Fox, "Joe Millionaire" breaks the ratings bank. *USA Today*. Retrieved from http://usatoday30.usatoday.com/life/television/news/2003-02-18-joe-ratings_x.htm

Lipsky-Karasz, E. (2003, June 30). Faces & places: Reality world news of the week! *Us Weekly*, 12–13.

Longeretta, E. (2018, October 15). MTV's "The Hills" revival: Everything we know about "New Beginnings." *Us Weekly*. Retrieved from https://www.usmagazine.com/entertainment/pictures/the-hills-revival-everything-we-know-about-new-beginnings/

Lowenthal, L. (2006). Triumph of mass idols. In P. D. Marshall (Ed.), *The celebrity culture reader* (pp. 124–152). New York, NY, & London, UK: Routledge. (Original work published 1944).

Marshall, P. D. (2010). The promotion and presentation of the self: Celebrity as marker of presentational media. *Celebrity Studies, 1*(1), 35–48.

Marwick, A. (2013) *Status update: Celebrity, publicity and branding in the social media age*. New Haven, CT: Yale University Press.

Marwick, A., & boyd, d. (2011). To see and be seen: Celebrity practice on Twitter. *Convergence, 17*(2), 139–158.

McDonnell, A. (2014). *Reading celebrity gossip magazines*. Malden, MA: Polity.

McColgin, C. (2006, April 3). Is Kristin stealing Jessica's poses? *Us Weekly*, 56–57.

McColgin, C. (2006, October 2). Stylish black belts. *Us Weekly*, 6–7.

McColgin, C. (2007, May 7). Little white dresses. *Us Weekly*, 6–7.

McColgin, C. (2007, July 2). Who wore it best? *Us Weekly*, 6.

McColgin, C. (2007, September 24). Who wore it best? *Us Weekly*, 12.

McColgin, C. (2008, April 7). Who wore it best? *Us Weekly*, 4.

McColgin, C. (2008, August 4). Who wore it best? *Us Weekly*, 6.

McCracken, E. (1993). *Decoding women's magazines: From "Mademoiselle" to "Ms."* London, UK: MacMillan Press.

McRobbie, A. (2004). Post-feminism and popular culture. *Feminist Media Studies, 4*(3), 255–264.

Mehalic, J. (2004, September 6). Meet the new bachelors! *Us Weekly*, 62.

Meneses, M. (2008, September 29). Lauren's Emmy design. *Us Weekly*, 78–79.

Meneses, M. (2009, October 19). Audrina's mini marathon. *Us Weekly*, 2–3.

Meyers, E. (2010) Reality television and the hypertrophic celebrity in *Victoria Beckham: Coming to America. Celebrity Studies 1*(3), 319–333.

Meyers, E. (2011). Gossip blogs and "baby bumps": The new visual spectacle of female celebrity in gossip media. In K. Ross (Ed.), *The handbook of gender, sex and media* (pp. 53–70). Oxford, UK: Wiley-Blackwell Publishing.

Meyers, E. (2013). *Dishing dirt in the digital age: Celebrity gossip blogs and participatory media culture.* New York, NY: Peter Lang.

Milter, J. (2001, May 21). Is there life after *Survivor*? *Us Weekly*, 35.

Min, J. (2017, March 16). 25 Things You Didn't Know About . . . *Us Weekly*. Retrieved from https://www.buzzfeednews.com/article/janicemin/things-you-didnt-know-about-us-weekly MTV Movie magic! (2007, June 18). *Us Weekly*, 44–45.

Nielsen. (2011, September 21). 10 years of primetime the rise of reality and sports programming. Retrieved from http://www.nielsen.com/us/en/insights/news/2011/10-years-of-primetime-the-rise-of-reality-and-sports-programming.html

A night out with *Us*. (2009, May 11). *Us Weekly*, 18–19.

O'Leary, K. (2006, March 27). Another secret date. *Us Weekly*, 50–53.

O'Leary, K. (2008, December 8). Heidi and Spencer: Yes, we eloped! *Us Weekly*, 46–53.

Ouelette, L., & Murray, S. (2004). Introduction. In S. Murray & L. Ouellette (Eds.), *Reality TV: Remaking television culture* (pp. 1–15). New York, NY: New York University Press.

Pappas, B. (2000, September 18) The survivor. *Us Weekly*, 54–59.

Pappas, B. (2001, January 29). *Survivor II. Us Weekly*, 45–51.

Pappas, B. (2001, May 21a). Survival of the nicest. *Us Weekly*, 28–35.

Pappas, B. (2001, May 21b). What was beneath all that sunshine? *Us Weekly*, 32–33.

Pappas, B. (2001, May 21c). A happy afterlife for America's sweetheart. *Us Weekly*, 34–35.

Pappas, B. (2003, February 24). The future Mrs. Millionaire? *Us Weekly*, 49.

Pappas, B. (2003, March 31). Bring on *The Bachelor* 3. *Us Weekly*, 46–47.

Pappas, B. (2003, June 2) The Bachelor & Jen: Our love story. *Us Weekly*, 44.

Pappas, B. (2003, November 3). Reality revelations: What the women don't know about Bob. *Us Weekly*, 56–57.

Pappas, B., & Hong, C. (2002, May 13). *The Bachelor*! His nude scene (maybe), their love future (yes) & more. *Us Weekly*, 44–45.

Pérez-Peña, R. (2008, February 11). 2 celebrity magazines buck circulation trend. *The New York Times*. Retrieved from https://www.nytimes.com/2008/02/11/business/media/11cnd-mag.html

Petersen, A. H. (2011). Towards an industrial history of celebrity gossip: *The National Enquirer, People Magazine*, and "personality journalism" in the 1970s. *Celebrity Studies*, 2(2), 131–149.

Ponce de Leon, C. L. (2002). *Self-exposure: Human-interest journalism and the emergence of celebrity in America, 1890–1940*. Chapel Hill, NC, & London, UK: University of North Carolina Press.

Ratledge, I. (2003, July 7–14). Evan's 16th minute of fame. *Us Weekly*, 6.

Ratledge, I. (2003, November 10). Trista's wedding dress dreams! *Us Weekly*, 52–53.

Redmond, S. (2014). *Celebrity and the media*. London, UK, & New York, NY: Palgrave Macmillan.

Rehn, T. (2003, February 24). *The Bachelorette*'s Diary. *Us Weekly*, 72.

Reinstein, M. (2003, December 22). Trista & Ryan's wedding: What the cameras didn't catch. *Us Weekly*, 54–55.

Reinstein, M. (2005, May 30). A dream wedding. *Us Weekly*, 56–59.

Reinstein, M. (2008, March 17). How Spencer betrayed me. *Us Weekly*, 54–59.

Reinstein, M., & Sóuter, E. (2009, June 1). From mom . . . to monster. *Us Weekly*, 64–76.

Rojek, C. (2001). *Celebrity*. London, UK: Reaktion Books.

Rutenberg, J., Ruiz, R. R., & Protess, B. (2018, August 23). David Pecker, chief of National Enquirer's publisher, is said to get immunity in Trump inquiry. *The New York Times*. Retrieved from https://www.nytimes.com/2018/08/23/us/politics/david-pecker-immunity-trump.html

Sconce, J. (2007). A vacancy at the Paris Hilton. In J. Gray, C. Sandvoss, & C. L. Harrington (Eds.), *Fandom: Identities and communities in a mediated world* (pp. 328–343). New York: New York University Press.

Senft, T. (2008). *Camgirls: Celebrity and community in the age of social networks*. New York, NY: Peter Lang.

Sharpe, L. (Producer). (2017, March 22). Revisiting the glory days of *Us Weekly* [Interview with the former deputy managing editor Amy Vinciguerra]. *Dirtcast* [Audio podcast]. Retrieved from https://jezebel.com/revisiting-the-glory-days-of-us-weekly-1793521248

Snider, M. (2017, March 15) "National Enquirer" parent buys "Us Weekly" from Wenner Media. *USA Today*. Retrieved from https://www.usatoday.com/story/money/business/2017/03/15/ national-enquirer-parent-buys-us-weekly-wenner-media/99232236/

Souter, E. (2009, October 12). Kristin's true crimes. *Us Weekly*, 64–66.

Stableford, D. (2008, February 11). Magazines take a huge hit at the newsstand. *Folio*. Retrieved from: https://www.foliomag.com/magazines-take-hit-newsstand/

Stack, T. (2008, August 8). They shoot. She scores. *Entertainment Weekly*, pp. 26–28.

Stars party with *Us*. (2007, October 15). *Us Weekly*, 26–27.

Stelter, B. (2008, March 27). "The Hills" draws 4.8 million on TV, 1.8 million online. *The New York Times*. Retrieved July 26, 2018, from https://mediadecoder.blogs.nytimes.com/2008/03/27/ the-hills-draws-48-million-on-tv-18-million-online/

Sternheimer, K. (2011). *Celebrity culture and the American dream: Stardom and social mobility*. New York, NY: Routledge.

Story, L. (2005, June 13). Forget about milk and bread. Give me gossip! *The New York Times*, p. C1.

Tegnelia, A. (2003, March 31). Life after *Joe*. *Us Weekly*, 32.

Tegnelia, A., & Youngman, S. (2003, June 16). Faces & places: Diva doings. *Us Weekly*, 10–11.

TheLittleMarket. (March 8, 2017). The story behind The Little Market [Blog post]. *Cultural Exchange: The Little Market*. Retrieved from http://blog.thelittlemarket.com/the-story-behind-the-little-market/

Tomczak, S. (2004, November 1). Faces & places: World news of the week! *Us Weekly*, 18–19.

Turner, G. (2004). *Understanding celebrity*. London, UK, & Thousand Oaks, CA: Sage.

Turner, G. (2010). Approaching celebrity studies. *Celebrity Studies*, *1*(1), 11–20.

Turner, G. (2014). Reality television and the demotic turn. In L. Ouellette (Ed.), *A companion to reality television* (pp. 309–323). Malden, MA: John Wiley & Sons.

Us Buzzzz-o-meter. (2008, February 18). *Us Weekly*, 87.

Van Krieken, R. (2012). *Celebrity society*. New York, NY: Routledge.

Warner, K. J. (2017). In the time of plastic representation. *Film Quarterly*, *71*(2). Retrieved from https://filmquarterly.org/2017/12/04/in-the-time-of-plastic-representation/

Weber, L., & Finger, B. (2017, May 4). What we lose if we lose *Us Weekly*. *Vanity Fair*. Retrieved from https://www.vanityfair.com/style/2017/05/us-weekly-wenner-ami-sale

The week. (2006, August 14). *Advertising Age*, *77*(33), 14.

Where other stars wed, (2005, July 25). *Us Weekly*, 68–69.

Wilson, J. A. (2010). Star testing: The emerging politics of celebrity gossip. *The Velvet Light Trap*, *65*, 25–38.

Wilson, J. A. (2014) Reality television celebrity: Star consumption and self-production in media culture. In L. Ouellette (Ed.), *A companion to reality television* (pp. 421–436). Malden, MA: John Wiley & Sons.

WNYC Studios (Producer). (2018, March 13). The turnaround artist: Janice Min on magazines and #MeToo. *Here's the thing with Alec Baldwin* [Audio podcast]. Retrieved from https://www.wnycstudios.org/story/turnaround-artist-janice-min-us-weekly-and-hollywood-reporter

Youngman, S. (2003, June 9). Their first week together: *Bachelor* shocker! There is no prenup! *Us Weekly*, 50.

INDEX

Page numbers in italics refer to figures.

ABOUT THE AUTHOR

Erin A. Meyers is an associate professor of communication at Oakland University. Her first book, *Dishing Dirt in the Digital Age: Celebrity Gossip Blogs and Participatory Media Culture* (2013), explored the influence of gossip blogs on contemporary celebrity culture. She is currently the coeditor of *Celebrity Studies*.